REVIEWS OF
NATIONAL POLICIES
FOR EDUCATION

SPAIN

ORGANISATION FOR ECONOMIC CO-OPERATION AND DEVELOPMENT

Pursuant to article 1 of the Convention signed in Paris on 14th December, 1960, and which came into force on 30th September, 1961, the Organisation for Economic Co-operation and Development (OECD) shall promote policies designed:

- to achieve the highest sustainable economic growth and employment and a rising standard of living in Member countries, while maintaining financial stability, and thus to contribute to the development of the world economy;
- to contribute to sound economic expansion in Member as well as non-member countries in the process of economic development; and
- to contribute to the expansion of world trade on a multilateral, non-discriminatory basis in accordance with international obligations.

The Signatories of the Convention on the OECD are Austria, Belgium, Canada, Denmark, France, the Federal Republic of Germany, Greece, Iceland, Ireland, Italy, Luxembourg, the Netherlands, Norway, Portugal, Spain, Sweden, Switzerland, Turkey, the United Kingdom and the United States. The following countries acceded subsequently to this Convention (the dates are those on which the instruments of accession were deposited): Japan (28th April, 1964), Finland (28th January, 1969), Australia (7th June, 1971) and New Zealand (29th May, 1973).

The Socialist Federal Republic of Yugoslavia takes part in certain work of the OECD (agreement of 28th October, 1961).

Publié en français sous le titre:

EXAMENS DES
POLITIQUES NATIONALES D'ÉDUCATION
ESPAGNE

This review of educational policy in Spain took place some ten years after the end of the Franquiste regime that had stifled educational development for almost four decades. Today, freedom, participation, devolution and creative enterprise have become guiding concepts in accelerating the political, social and economic development of the nation. In that development education has been assigned a central place.

The examiners note that Spain is launched upon the implementation of a formidable array of reforms affecting virtually every aspect of the education system. They wonder whether all the reforms can be implemented effectively within the foreseeable future, particularly in view of the necessity for increased capital expenditure on buildings and equipment and a heavy investment in pre-service and in-service teacher training. Should there not be, they ask, a hierarchy of priorities? And is there not a strong case for indicative overall planning?

A striking feature of the current educational scene in Spain is the speed at which powers historically concentrated at the centre in Madrid are being devolved to the regions, which are designated "Autonomous Regions" (*comunidades autónomas*). The intention is to encourage democratic decision-making and to ensure that future reforms answer to the real local needs. The examiners believe that this is highly desirable but caution that decentralisation should not be allowed to lead to inequalities of resources and educational opportunities between the regions. This might happen if effective machinery is not put in place for reconciling nation-wide with regional priorities. For their part the Spanish authorities are insistent that inequalities will not arise; for example, candidates for universities will be able to go to the institution of their choice and teachers will be able to move from one province to another.

On schools, the examiners raise a multitude of issues. Their overriding concern, however, is with reform of secondary education. What must be done to raise the quality of lower secondary education and to reduce the high terminal failure rate of 35 per cent of the age group? Can the achievements among the major experimental programmes now under way be replicated throughout the country?

As in the rest of the OECD family the upper secondary level is currently causing a great deal of heartsearching. The academic track is prestigious but saddled with an out-of-date curriculum. The vocational track is held in low esteem and suffers from a severe lack of resources. The report discusses the advantages of moving towards a comprehensive education and training system and the Spanish authorities themselves are disposed to adopt a more flexible model and an up-to-date curriculum.

On universities, the examiners note that Spain had experienced a massive expansion of enrolment over a very short space of time with consequential pressures on teaching and material resources as well as a high rate of student wastage or drop-out during the initial years of study. Their questions mostly concern ways and means of increasing the graduation success rate while also developing the universities' research role, which is at present weak.

The review leaves no doubt that, in pursuing its educational goals, Spain has three invaluable assets. The first is the high esteem in which the newly-established democratic system of education is held by the public. The second is the realism of the majority of policy-makers, administrators and teachers. The third asset is the youthfulness of so many of the decision-makers and administrators and of a large majority of the teachers at all levels.

A record of the review meeting, which contains full replies to all the examiners' questions, constitutes Part Two of this volume and Part Three comprises a synthesis of the Spanish authorities' Background Report.

Also available

REVIEW OF NATIONAL POLICIES FOR EDUCATION:

ITALY – Educational Reforms (May 1985)
(91 85 01 1) ISBN 92-64-12702-X   112 pages   £7.50   US$15.00   F75.00   DM33.00

PORTUGAL (April 1984)
(91 84 01 1) ISBN 92-64-12568-X   110 pages   £6.00   US$12.00   F60.00   DM27.00

NEW ZEALAND (August 1983)
(91 83 04 1) ISBN 92-64-12477-2   140 pages   £6.60   US$13.00   F66.00   DM30.00

FINLANDE (October 1982)
(91 82 03 2) ISBN 92-64-22371-1   138 pages   £6.60   US$13.00   F66.00   DM33.00
English text: "Finland" .... Out of print

GREECE (July 1982)
(91 82 02 1) ISBN 92-64-12334-2   122 pages   £4.50   US$9.00   F45.00   DM23.00

YUGOSLAVIA (January 1982)
(91 82 01 1) ISBN 92-64-12270-2   152 pages   £4.30   US$9.50   F43.00   DM22.00

SWEDEN – Educational Reforms (March 1981)
(91 81 03 1) ISBN 92-64-12150-1   108 pages   £3.20   US$8.00   F32.00   DM16.00

UNITED STATES – Federal Policies for Education for the Disadvantaged (February 1981)
(91 81 02 1) ISBN 92-64-12149-8   128 pages   £3.40   US$8.50   F34.00   DM17.00

DENMARK (June 1980)
(91 80 03 1) ISBN 92-64-12071-8   162 pages   £4.70   US$10.50   F42.00   DM21.00

Prices charged at the OECD Bookshop.

*THE OECD CATALOGUE OF PUBLICATIONS and supplements will be sent free of charge
on request addressed either to OECD Publications Service, Sales and Distribution Division,
2, rue André-Pascal, 75775 PARIS CEDEX 16, or to the OECD Sales Agent in your country.*

TABLE OF CONTENTS

Part One
THE EXAMINERS' REPORT

Part Two
RECORD OF THE REVIEW MEETING
Paris, 5th December 1985

Part Three
THE SPANISH EDUCATION SYSTEM

THE OECD EXAMINERS

Professor J.R. FRAUSTO DA SILVA — Director, The National Institute of Administration, former Minister of Education, Portugal

Dr. M. MILUTINOVIĆ — Director, The National Library, former Minister of Education, Serbia, Yugoslavia

Professor P. VANBERGEN — Former Secretary-General, Ministry of Education, French-speaking sector, Belgium

THE SPANISH DELEGATION

Mr. José Maria MARAVALL — Minister of Education and Science (Head of the Delegation)

H.E. Mr. José-Vicente TORRENTE — Ambassador, Permanent Representative to the OECD

Mr. Joaquin ARANGO — Secretary-General for Education

Mr. Emilio LAMO DE ESPINOSA — Secretary-General, Council of the Universities

Mr. José SEGOVIA — Director General for Post-compulsory Secondary Education

Mr. Manuel SOUTO — Director General for Planning and Investments

Mr. Julio CARABAÑA — Director, National Centre of Educational Research and Documentation (CIDE)

Mr. Miguel Angel de FRUTOS — Attaché, Permanent Delegation to the OECD

Mr. Miguel BARROSO — Head of the Press Department, Office of the Minister of Education and Science

Mr. José M. COSTA — Vice-General Directorate for International Cooperation

Part One

THE EXAMINERS' REPORT

I

A NEW ROLE FOR EDUCATION

The wider setting

Spain is physically the second largest country in Western Europe with a total area of 504 800 Km², including the Balearic and Canary islands. Its overall population of 38 173 000 is, however, more sparsely dispersed than in many other countries at 76 per Km². At the same time, there is a high concentration of population in the large conurbations : for example, 60 per cent of the 6 million population of Catalonia are concentrated in and around Barcelona. Both internal and external migration, which had been on a large scale for many years, have now subsided to a trickle.

During the past decade there has been a marked decline in the birth rate which, now at 13.4 per thousand, is about the average for OECD countries. As elsewhere, the percentage of retired people is increasing rapidly. Thus, in the future the education system will be concerned with a diminishing relative population of children and young people and the consequences of a general upward shift in the age bracket.

Spain's top priority is rapid economic expansion and to this end it has embarked on a policy of austerity to bring down what was a high rate of inflation. Spanish gross domestic product for 1984 has been estimated at US 158.15 billion, representing US 4 137 per capita at current exchange rates. GDP increased annually by about 1 per cent between 1978 and 1983, but fell by 2.25 per cent in 1983-84. Although per capita income has been growing, it still remains relatively low. Furthermore, this average figure masks sharp disparities between the richest and poorest regions. Significantly, for the education sector, expenditure on research and development (0.4 per cent of GDP) is one of the lowest among OECD countries, a fact to which the examiners will return in a subsequent chapter.

In short, the present condition of the Spanish economy is highly complex and poses a challenge to the national authorities : to contain inflation and then steadily reduce it while achieving 5 per cent annual growth ; to cut the balance of payments deficit ; to reduce the public sector ; to carry out industrial reorganisation ; to create a more flexible labour market. The challenge is daunting. It is no longer possible to postpone structural changes in the entire economy, and this will require the economic system to be both highly adaptable and efficient.

The most pressing problem is the high rate of unemployment and the severe restructuring problems to which that gives rise. The national average was running at about 20 per cent in 1984, but there are areas where the rate is much higher. A sizable percentage of the inactive population consists of early school-leavers seeking their first employment. Even though the presence of a large hidden labour market mitigates the reality of official unemployment statistics, the fact remains that Spain has the second highest rate of unemployment among OECD countries and creating jobs is, therefore, a national priority. As we shall see, the unemployment factor explains much of the demand for more education and the authorities' concern to raise the level of occupational skills.

Apart from the closing of the migration safety-valve, one reason for the severe unemployment level has been the modernisation of agriculture and the unusually rapid drift from rural areas to the towns and cities, especially on the part of the young. At the beginning of the twentieth century approximately 70 per cent of the population lived off the land. That percentage is now down to 15 per cent, though it must be noted that 312 000 Km^2 of the land is still agricultural and of that 204 900 Km^2 are being tilled. Industrial employment absorbs 33.5 per cent of the total (estimate for 1985). The big increase in employment, as generally in OECD countries, has been in the service sector, which now accounts for 48.4 per cent of the workforce. Over one million people are employed in the tourist trade alone, international tourism contributing 4.3 per cent of GDP in 1984, the second highest share among OECD countries. Fishing continues to be a key occupation, employing directly or indirectly some two million people. Altogether, 18 per cent of the active population is now employed in agriculture, forestry and fishing.

Table 1.   ACTIVE POPULATION IN THE DIFFERENT ECONOMIC SECTORS

Per cent

Year	Agriculture	Industry/Construction	Other
1940	50.5	22.1	27.3
1960	39.7	32.9	27.3
1984	18.2	35.2	46.6

During the period 1942 to 1984 the population increased from 26.3 millions to 38.2 millions, of which the potential active population is about 14 millions. Curiously enough, the parallel growth in GNP of some 400 per cent was obtained by practically the same working population, at least after 1960.

Table 2.   VARIATION IN WORKING POPULATION 1960-1984

Thousands

1960	1972	1978	1984
11 676	12 458	12 081	10 638

Migration from Spain to other countries is a time-honoured tradition. Millions of Spaniards have settled permanently abroad, though maintaining close ties with the homeland. Links with Latin America are intimate and now sedulously cultivated. Many Spaniards are living and working temporarily in other European countries – notably, France, Germany and Switzerland – though a major return to Spain has taken place within the last few years.

All the geographical, economic and social factors briefly described so far are relevant to the current concerns of the education system. Other factors must also be mentioned. The first

10

is the continuing strength of the family unit in Spain, which ensures not only good care of the young, but of the old as well. The examiners visited several schools where the school meal canteen facilities were largely or totally unused, the reason given being that families preferred to assemble together at home for lunch. They also noticed the easy relationship between children and adults, which appeared to be based on mutual trust.

The second factor is linguistic pluralism. Catalan is spoken not only in Catalonia but also in the Balearics and Valencia. Euskera is spoken in the Basque region. Gallego is spoken in a few parts of Asturias, Leon and Zamora as well as in Galicia itself. In Asturias the dialect "Bable" is spoken. Instruction in the traditional language in the Basque region, Catalonia, and Galicia places a heavy but ineluctable burden on the curriculum and the supply of texts. It also raises a difficulty for the curriculum in finding adequate time for teaching a foreign language. Many Spanish children are now expected to master in effect three languages : the historic regional language, Castillan, and English or French.

The importance of language learning is connected with a third factor of enormous importance for Spain – its accession to the European Economic Community – an event that occurred as the examiners were writing their report. Spain has great expectations of this new union, while being fully aware that high risks as well as large gains are at stake. For education and training it poses even more acutely the already perceived necessity of bringing achievement levels up to West European norms.

A challenging role for education

Spain is physically cut off from Europe by the Pyrenees and until recently was governed autocratically from the centre in relative cultural as well as geographical isolation, except from Latin America. Internally, it is segmented geographically into distinct regions or provinces that have never lost their own cultures and, in some instances, their own language. So we are looking at an education system that must harmonize the needs of distinctive regional identities with those of a nationwide culture that, more than in most countries, has resisted the standardizing effects of mass consumption, mass communications, advanced technology and travel. Public education was failing to achieve that harmonization until very recently. Highly centralised, woefully short of resources, static, and reflecting the idea of a dominant national culture throughout the long period of the Franco regime, it did not command the full support or the esteem of the regions.

In a remarkably short space of time there has been a dramatic turn-around. Democratic institutions and processes have been restored. Freedom, participation and devolution have become guiding concepts. And education is seen to have a leading role to play in the consolidation of democracy.

Indeed, the most striking feature of the educational scene today is the deliberate transfer of responsibilities from the centre to the regions ; significantly, the word "regions" is now usually qualified by the adjective "autonomous". Six regions – Andalusia, Basque, Catalonia, Galicia, Valencia and the Canary Islands – already enjoy more or less educational independence as will the other eleven provinces in due course. The transfer of powers affects the whole of social administration and to some degree economic administration as well. However, it is commonly recognized that no sector of policy-making and control will be more affected than education, which will be very largely directed by the respective regions within less than five years' time.

The new distribution of powers will not transform Spain constitutionally from a unitary to a federal State, but it will give something like home rule to the regions and create an entirely new set of political relationships. In a comparative perspective, the intriguing question for education is whether policy-making and control will most resemble the American, Australian, German or, say, Yugoslav model. Many issues have to be resolved including the following : What will be the future scope of the jurisdiction of the Ministry of Education and what specific functions will the Ministry retain ? What will be the size and structure of the reformed Ministry ? What will be the links between the central Ministry and the ministries in the autonomous regions ? How will education be financed ? What arrangements will be made to assist the educational development of the poorer regions of the country ? To what extent will uniformity of curriculum and pupil assessment be secured ? Will Spain be influenced at all by other country models of decentralised education ?

To devolve educational powers from Madrid to the regional capitals will be one thing ; to devolve powers from the latter to local communities and schools will be another. The vital question is whether in practice education will be liberated from the excessive rules and regulations – so many and so complicated that they were often ineffectual – that have stifled initiative in the past. In short, will local community and school-based development be encouraged ? We intend to offer our own thoughts on these critical issues in Chapter III.

THE EDUCATION SYSTEM

Spectacular expansion of education

Until very recently many children of school age were not attending school, and the lycées (grammar schools) and universities catered for a small elite. In the last years of the former regime, and particularly since the return of democracy, an egalitarian philosophy has dominated educational thinking and policies. The result is that, today, virtually all children attend compulsory school, 85 per cent of the 5-year age group are in pre-school establishments, the retention rate in secondary education is very high and still increasing, and the universities are no longer providing education for an elite but for a substantial percentage of young people in the immediate post-secondary school age group. School enrolments at the beginning of the year 1984-85 were 5.6 million, including 220 000 new places. To all intents and purposes, the demand for education is being fully satisfied, except in the pre-primary and upper-secondary sectors.

This expansion has been more spectacular than in any other OECD country, which is stating a great deal in view of the expansionist surge that has occurred almost everywhere. It has entailed appointing tens of thousands of new teachers (ten thousand for 1984-85 alone) and sustaining an intensive building programme. Not surprisingly, the quality of educational provision has been, and remains, as a result most uneven in terms of teacher effectiveness, adequacy of buildings and equipment and availability of learning aids. The gap between extremes is disturbing. The authorities are anxious to raise standards in poorer schools and to bring up the general level of achievement in all schools. Part of our task, as we see it, is to offer suggestions as to how this may be done.

The education sectors

Pre-schooling is regarded as a high educational priority, though there is no intention of lowering the compulsory starting age. The demand for places exceeds the supply in many urban school districts.

Compulsory schooling lasts eight years (from age 6 to 14) and since 1981 has been divided into three cycles : initial = 1-2 ; middle = 3-5 ; higher 6-8. The school year runs from 1 September to 30 June and the day spans five hours, usually 9-12 and 3-5. The legal maximum class size is 40. In inner city areas the average size is 30-35 ; in rural areas it is much lower.

Coeducation, introduced only twenty years ago, is the rule, except in a few private schools. The intention is that physically and mentally handicapped children should be integrated into normal schools, except when suffering from a particularly grave disability, but for the time being most of them remain in special schools.

Secondary education is divided into two branches : a) preparation for the baccalaureat (Bachillerato Unificado Polivalente) ; b) vocational education and training. The former, which is open to pupils with an EGB certificate, consists of three years of general studies and a fourth year for specific university preparation. Options are essentially closed from the end of the third year. The second branch consists of two levels : i) a two- or three-year course after EGB ; ii) a three-year course, which may also be taken by students who have completed the BUP.

A large percentage of schooling in Spain (36 per cent) *is private*. Most of the private schools are located in cities and no fewer than 66 per cent of pupils in Barcelona and 50 per cent in Madrid attend them. Up to 85 per cent of each private school's expenditure, based on the total number of student enrolments, is financed by the State. Private schools follow the same curriculum as the public schools.

Sixty thousand young Spaniards of school age are *living abroad*. This might seem a small number, but it greatly concerns the Ministry of Education, which, like several other education ministries in Europe, is committed to ensuring that children living abroad shall not lose their national identity and shall be able, with relative ease, to reintegrate into a school in Spain should their families return home.

In recent years Spain has experienced an explosion in the number of students entering *higher education*. There is no *numerus clausus* and each student is allowed to go to the university of his or her choice subject to the availability of appropriate facilities, such as laboratory places. There are now 25 public universities together with a "Distance" (or Open) University, and four private universities. The student population leapt from 100 000 in 1965 to 354 000 in 1970. In 1984-85 it was approximately 750 000, more than double the 1970 total. At one secondary school in a *working class* suburb of Barcelona we were told that 75 per cent of those finishing school intended to go on to university. The question is, of course, whether the country can afford such high participation in university-level studies.

The *education of adults* is a high priority, with a view to eliminating adult illiteracy. At present, there are two million illiterate adults and an estimated eleven million functionally illiterate (an estimate which appears to us questionably high).

The much improved level of education across the nation is shown in Table 4. Although over 30 per cent of the population over the age of 10 has no school qualification (Table 3), only about 8 per cent are illiterate and the majority of these are of advanced age. At the same time, only 7.38 per cent of the population has completed the full cycle of schooling (BUP or FP – vocational education) and only 6 per cent higher or post-secondary-level education, percentages which would appear too low if the economy is to expand faster. It is also to be noted that the percentages of those with degrees from university schools (short cycle) and university faculties (long cycle) are virtually similar. That distortion will tend to increase in the years to come as can be seen by the distribution of students among the various educational levels.

13

Diagram of the education system

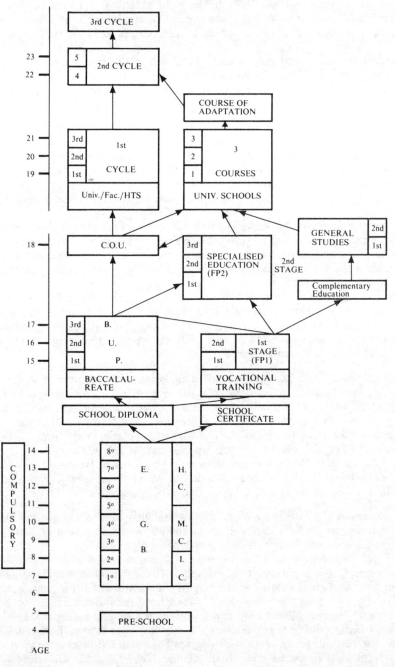

Source: *España: Desarrollo de la educación en 1981-83,* Ministerio de Educación y Ciencia, Geneva, 1984, p. 434.

14

Table 3. DISTRIBUTION OF THE POPULATION
ACCORDING TO EDUCATIONAL LEVEL

10 years onwards, no longer studying in per cent

Illiterates	7.92
No level reached	23.05
Primary (initial + middle) school	42.42
Lower secondary EGB	12.15
Upper secondary (general education and vocational tracks)	7.38
University schools	3.64
University faculties	3.04
Non classified	0.4

Source: 1981 Census.

Table 4. NUMBER OF STUDENTS
IN THE VARIOUS EDUCATIONAL LEVELS (1982-83)

Level	Students
Pre-school	1 187 600
EGB	5 633 500
BUP/COU (upper secondary general)	1 117 600
FP1 and FP2 (upper secondary vocational)	650 900
Various upper secondary level	388 600
University schools	181 800
Faculties and University colleges	464 600
Higher technical schools	45 800
Various post-secondary level	36 900

Educational assets

In pursuing its educational goals Spain has three invaluable assets. The first is the high esteem in which the newly-established democratic system of education is held by the public. Despite critical shortages, despite the realisation that rapid expansion has created tough problems, despite the poor job prospects of school-leavers, the public generally approves of education and parents are very largely satisfied with their children's schools. The second is the realism of the majority of policy-makers, administrators and teachers. They recognize that Rome was not built in a day, are quick themselves to point out the deficiencies of the system and readily listen to the views of such outsiders as a team of OECD examiners. The third asset is the youthfulness of so many of the decision-makers and administrators and of a large majority of the teachers at all levels. If the enthusiasm of these young actors in the educational enterprise can be effectively mobilised, the auguries for the future are more than promising.

In succeeding chapters we propose first to consider educational policies and priorities at the national and local level together with the financial and other obstacles to be overcome. We shall then analyse the chief problems of each sector of the system – compulsory (or basic), upper secondary, including training, and post-secondary. Two chapters will deal, respectively, with some specific school issues, and policies for training and retraining teachers. The last chapter will be devoted to higher education.

II

POLICY-MAKING, PLANNING AND FINANCING

The policy-making process

The national education authorities are as clear about the operational difficulties of implementing their policies as they are about what they want to achieve. Of one reality they are quite convinced, namely, the futility of preparing and promulgating elaborate laws in the abstract and postulating a global reform. Such laws read majestically but take an inordinate amount of time to prepare and filter through the legislative process and in the event often have little effect, thereby giving rise to frustrated expectations and cynicism about the value of subsequent grand designs. Global reform "has been replaced by gradual and systematic revision of the different levels and educational models, with a different reach and orientation for each of them"[1]. So, the Spanish authorities have elected to proceed by means of pilot experiments. A law should be enacted, they consider, only when structural and procedural plans for reform have been drawn up that experimentation has shown likely to work.

Another new facet is the placing of education within the framework of national goals and development projections. In the past, education existed within a closed and relatively unchanging universe. Now it is expected to contribute positively to overall plans for national economic growth and social improvement. This can be seen by perusing, for example, a study on educational reform recently written by the Minister of Education himself. In its pages the Minister designates for education a far-reaching role in the social, cultural and economic life of the nation [2].

It is, of course, always easy to state, on the one hand, the necessity of integrating educational policy with economic and social development, but notoriously difficult, on the other, to bring about that integration in practice. The difficulty is compounded in Spain by the devolution of educational powers to the regions that is the subject of the next chapter. Our impression is that the intention in Spain is resolute but that the reality of integration is far from being achieved. Above all, there is the tricky problem of establishing close inter-ministerial relations that we shall describe below.

The question of priorities

The reform plans comprise several priorities, four of which are strongly emphasized in public documents and pronouncements:

- *i)* a horizontal and vertical extension of pre-school education;
- *ii)* reform of the lower secondary cycle (forms 6 to 8) which will entail heavy expenditure on teaching materials and equipment and a huge retraining programme for teachers;

iii) reform of the first two years of the upper secondary cycle (forms 9 to 10) that will entail not only a huge retraining programme for teachers and heavy expenditure on teaching materials and equipment, but substantial capital investment as well;

iv) reform of higher education.

Moreover, these reforms will lead to an increase, first, in 14-16 age group enrolments and then, very soon afterwards, an increase in 17-18 age group enrolments. It is difficult, therefore, to see how all the authorities' priorities can be pursued simultaneously.

Another problem with regard to ordering priorities concerns the effects of the decentralisation process. Formation by the Autonomous Regions of their own educational policies may lead to tensions, if not conflicts, between priorities set at the national level and priorities set by them, given that such salient factors as the percentage of illiterates, levels of instruction and demographic trends are not everywhere the same. This points to the necessity of creating administrative and financial mechanisms that will permit continuous adjustment of divergent priorities.

The examiners were unable to discern the processes by which priorities are ranked. This may well be because the appropriate machinery does not exist or because the national authorities prefer to keep their options wide open and to pursue several priorities simultaneously.

Consultation and consensus

It is the desire of the authorities that the interests of school and society should coincide, that employers and unions should participate in the consultative and decision-making process. The examiners did not gain the impression, however, that a regular system of consultation has been sufficiently developed either at national or local level. That is not to say that the national Ministry of Education does not inform the public about its plans and intentions. On the contrary, the Minister of Education and spokesmen of the Ministry are obviously at pains to explain and discuss their policies and problems in complete frankness through the media. The Press, for example, devotes considerable space to educational matters.

Our concern is rather with the need to establish broadly representative consultative bodies at all levels which can serve as sources of advice and sounding-boards for educational policy-makers. We do not go so far as to recommend including at once the function of monitoring the performance of the education system but in the longer term Spain, like many OECD countries in the present epoch, may find it desirable, or even imperative, to create effective participatory machinery for rendering the education system accountable to society for all its actions. As far as we could ascertain the National Schooling Board does not perform such a function.

Role of a national inspectorate

Spain has long had in place a nation-wide general inspectorate of the traditional kind for the several educational levels. The present administration is still considering, however, what precise role to prescribe for it in the future against the background of the judgement expressed in the Background Report: "Various attempts have been made to establish a General Inspectorate of Public Instruction but have had little effect. Owing to successive obstacles which were of a diverse nature, the project was doomed to failure" (page 47). The delay in arriving at a decision is presumably largely explained by the necessity of waiting for the devolution process to be completed, for this, logically, ought to lead to many of the customary and day-to-day inspectorial tasks being carried out within what amount to regional education systems and to inspectors being answerable to the regional authorities. We also suspect that the existing inspectorate may be considered too set in the ways of the old static system to function as flexibly and imaginatively as the reformed system will require. Nonetheless, it would seem to us that a national inspectorate of highly experienced education specialists will always be required and has potentially a richly creative role to play in disseminating information and stimulating innovations in educational practice and generally contributing to the nation-wide research and development effort.

Goals and guidelines

The Ministry of Education in Madrid issues curricular guidelines that are adapted by the regional authorities to fit in with their perception of actual needs and then issued as guidelines for implementation by the municipalities and local districts. We were informed by the authorities in the various autonomous regions that this system functions "surprisingly" well. No doubt it does in so far as the central and regional link is concerned. The essential question, however, is whether centrally and regionally inspired goals and guidelines make sense at the municipal and community level and, above all, in the schools. Our impression from school visits was that some teachers are by no means sure what they are expected to achieve or happy with the curriculum that they are required to offer. The lack of mutual understanding may have less to do with any ambiguity or rigidity in the guidelines than with the teachers' difficulty in perceiving their appropriateness to the specific school setting in which they happen to be working.

It is, of course, in the nature of things for teachers almost everywhere to feel that the guidelines and instructions they receive are unclear or arbitrary. Nevertheless, it would seem desirable to foresee in the implementation of reforms a stage for elucidating objectives and developing new texts for the use of administrators and teachers at the school and classroom level. Moreover, the scope for school-based initiatives has not yet been given serious attention. The examiners believe that a vigorous campaign should be launched designed to encourage principals and teachers to experiment with new curriculum and pedagogy in the light of their own perceptions of the needs of their own schools and pupils.

Planning and coordination

The formidable effort of the Spanish authorities to develop and sustain an all-embracing education system, covering pre-schooling to post-graduate studies and including vocational training and various forms of compensatory programmes, together with ambitious reform projects for almost every aspect of education, requires an equally formidable planning capacity both overall and sectorally, closely linked to the policy-making level and to the body or bodies in charge of research and development and evaluation. That capacity does not seem to exist or to be operational at the overall level and it is even more deficient at the sectoral level. The reform projects are not supported by adequate feasibility studies relating objectives to the resources required, and too much reliance appears to be placed on the political clout of the Minister or on the self-evident importance of the measures to ensure the necessary financial allocations in the annual bargaining process among ministries.

Coordination among the several sectors is inadequate and information exchanges are scarce among the different ministries. Examples of the lack of coordination can be observed in respect of the reform projects for the upper level of basic education and for the new 14-16 years-old cycle, carried out by groups of schools depending on different directorates which are not collaborating as closely as might be expected. The lack of interaction at the inter-ministerial level was revealed to the examiners by the fact that the Ministry of Labour is undertaking important inquiries on training and employment needs, which do not include the participation of, and, indeed, appeared to be unknown to, the Ministry of Education.

Interministerial coordination of policies not only at the political but also at the administrative and executive level is, therefore, an absolute necessity. At the present time when a radical change of the structure and content of vocational training is envisaged, it is axiomatic that the Ministry of Education should work in close collaboration with the Ministry of Labour, which has access to data and information crucial for the definition of targets as well as for the organisation and curriculum of the various programmes designed to provide training and lead to qualifications. If collaboration is found to be wanting and each Ministry implements its own schemes, a waste of resources, human, physical and financial, is bound to ensue and the opportunity to clarify the roles and respective competences of ministerial departments will be missed. This argument is valid for all intersectoral activities that cut across the vertical organisation of ministries, an obvious example being scientific research.

Although no formal body exists to coordinate the policies and programmes of the several ministries concerned with education and training, there is said to be close liaison on an *ad hoc* basis between the Ministry of Education and the Ministry of Planning. We believe that a standing body for coordinating policies and programmes in all ministries is called for, especially with regard to the reform of secondary education and the implementation of a rural development strategy.

Planning capacity

Throughout the many interviews and informal exchanges that occurred during their visit to Spain, the examiners were impressed by the competence of the top administrative and professional staff, by their grasp of problems and by the adequacy of the strategies applied in the various stages of experimentation in reform projects. At the same time, they were struck by the paucity of quantitative information about the human, physical and financial resources needed to implement plans within a reasonable time-schedule. Moreover, they detected a tendency to underestimate the difficulties and constraints that inevitably hamper the implementation of even the best conceived of plans and strategies.

Education planning, viewed internationally, has been criticized in recent years for offering insufficient and unreliable support for the policy and decision-making process because of the yawning gap between its predictions and eventual outcomes. This simply illustrates that some planning is not worth undertaking. It is far from implying that all planning is unnecessary. On the contrary, progressive organisations in all spheres, whether private or public, today regard planning as indispensable and are constantly testing new methods and instruments so as to overcome weaknesses and to give it a dynamic and adaptative character. In the examiners' opinion the planning capacity of the Spanish Ministry of Education ought to be greatly strengthened and perhaps blended with that of the CIDE (see below) or a similar body in order to dilute its technocratic bias. They are aware, of course, that planning is unfashionable at a time when political, ideological and regional pleadings carry so much weight. Even when a country's planning capacity is strong, to obtain substantial support for initiatives based exclusively on their merits against the equally legitimate claims of other social sectors, not to speak of those of the economically productive sector, is an uphill task, which cannot be expected to have continuous success throughout the extended period necessary for their implementation.

Financing

An essential fact should be noted about the constraints upon educational expenditure. This is the low rate of national taxation and consequential restricted national budget. Expenditure on education as a percentage of GDP at 3.5 per cent for 1984 Ministry of Education (2.7 per cent) and local authorities (0.8 per cent) is among the lowest within the OECD group of countries; total expenditure is about 30 per cent of GDP, which means that education absorbs almost 12 per cent of public expenditure. Arguably, of course, this low base gives Spain the possibility of considerable expansion provided that there be a powerful and continuing rise in economic output. It is certainly remarkable that, despite apparently cramped resources, Spain should have succeeded in erecting so many new educational buildings and recruiting so many new teachers at school and university over the past ten years. Moreover, the national education authorities do not believe that their reform plans are likely to falter for lack of appropriate financing; this partially explains their adoption of several priorities to be pursued in parallel, as we have already pointed out. Nor do they fear, as do Education Ministries in many other countries, that the Finance Ministry and the rest of the government are bent on keeping their expenditure within strict bounds.

The amount of public revenue available for education in all its forms is supplemented by the direct or indirect educational expenditures of other ministries, the Autonomous Regions, some local communities, employers, and private schools. The Ministries of Agriculture, Defence, Labour, Health and Social Security, in particular, spend a considerable amount on education, above all in the form of training. The autonomous provinces and municipalities also spend considerable sums. In Catalonia, for example, in 1983-84, city council expenditure was 5.7 per cent of the total expenditure for the region. As for employers, they appear to spend much less on training than in other countries. Even so, though exact details of their expenditures are not available, their contribution is still a significant factor. Finally, there is the expenditure of the private sector. Its contribution to school building stock is manifestly very great since it controls such a large proportion of the nation's schools (see Chapter VI). Its contribution to recurrent expenditure is less since the great majority of private schools receive up to 85 per cent of their annual costs, but it also remains a substantial amount. All in all, the real expenditure on education and training as a percentage of GDP is considerably higher than appears at first sight.

But the fundamental question in Spain is how can the authorities obtain sufficient resources to fund the broad array of reforms to which they are committed? The cost of extending the school-leaving age to sixteen alone will be great. The response of the authorities is that implementation of the major reforms will be gradual so as to permit parallel gradual increases in expenditure. We still believe that it would be helpful to develop more systematic forecasting of resource needs over the medium and long term.

Research and development

In Chapter I we drew attention to the very low rate of national expenditure on R&D for all purposes and in a subsequent chapter we shall comment on research expenditure within the university sector. Here we shall treat only of R&D as a key element in the policy-making, planning and educational reform process.

It is immediately conceded by the authorities that educational research has been historically very weak in Spain. There was no tradition to build on when the universities began to expand. Then, education departments were installed in each university. The teacher training colleges, though constituent parts of the universities (see Chapter VII), do not undertake research as one of their automatic functions and, in any case, do not for the most part have staff trained in research methods. There is a growing number of academics specialising in topics relevant to education but their output is small and not always related to pressing educational needs and problems. The examiners wonder whether the national authorities should not consider the possibility of funding a few departments of education as centres of excellence in educational research. They certainly believe that the training colleges should encourage their staff to undertake at least some research activities.

A valuable R&D instrument that is available to the Ministry of Education is the National Centre for Educational Research and Documentation (CIDE). This Centre has already carried out on its own account or commissioned many research inquiries. Its effectiveness, even with limited financial and personnel resources, has been demonstrated by the preparation of the Background Report for the present review, which assembles, collates and interprets a mass of statistical and descriptive information and contains many passages of penetrating policy analysis. The examiners wonder whether, given that additional resources can be found, its functions could not be enlarged so as to serve as the planning arm of the Minister of Education.

It will be necessary, of course, for each of the "Education Ministries" in the Autonomous Regions to acquire swiftly an R&D capacity. Meanwhile, appropriate consultative machinery needs to be constructed in parallel for harmonizing research activities between the Ministry of Education and the regions and among the regions themselves. We were informed that national plans for educational research are being prepared. This is undoubtedly essential if duplication is to be avoided and the research undertaken is to be relevant to national, regional or district needs.

NOTES AND REFERENCES

1. *España: Desarrollo de la educación en 1981-83*, Ministry of Education and Science, Geneva, 1984, p. 493.
2. José Maria Maravall, *La reforma de la enseñanza*, Laia Publishing House, Barcelona, 1984.

III

DECENTRALISATION AND REGIONALISATION

Regional autonomy and its consequences

The decentralisation of political power, decision-making and administrative structures or, as it is called, "the political decentralisation process", is one of those features of contemporary Spain which arouses admiration for its dynamism and comprehensive scope. It is also a process in which changes are taking place almost daily. Mechanisms that existed only a few months ago are already being modified or altered completely. For a country which, until the new Constitution was adopted in 1978, and more particularly since the signature of the Agreement on Regional Autonomy in 1981, was a highly centralised State, the establishment of Autonomous Regions endowed with wide powers and prerogatives is a major transformation that goes far towards meeting the long-standing democratic aspirations.

Although the country will remain unequivocally a unitary State in constitutional terms, its new political configuration with six regions ("historical" or full status regions) already autonomous and eleven more eventually to have partial or full autonomy, will render it more and more a pluralist society in practical political terms, if not a federation. It would be difficult now to halt a process of political devolution that is entirely appropriate for a country comprising several distinctive cultures and languages and having behind it a long and turbulent history of regional and communal affiliations crushed by a stifling central authority. To compare the new political order or at least its formal aspects (Autonomous Region Statutes) with existing federal or confederal countries (e.g. the United States, the Federal Republic of Germany, Switzerland or Yugoslavia) would be an unrewarding exercise. The really striking comparison is to be found between the Spain of today and Spain as it was barely ten years ago.

One vehicle of the dramatic transformation that is taking place is the education system, where decentralisation is now being steadily pursued. Indeed, although the transfer of power concerns social policy and to some extent economic policy as well, it is said that no sector of policy-making and administrative control will be more affected than education, which will be very largely directed by the respective regions within a five-year time horizon. It is recognised that even greater scope exists for the transfer of powers in education than at present provided for under the system of "shared responsibility". The notion of "shared responsibility" faces the central government and the Ministry of Education and Science on the one hand, and the Autonomous Region governments and education authorities on the other, with a great responsibility, for they must create the conditions in which a wide spectrum of citizens, parents, pupils, students, teachers, academics, research workers, civil servants, representatives of the

Arts, and not least trade unionists and representatives of industry, can be brought into a decision-making process that will affect future directions over the whole field of education. Powerful creative forces hitherto suppressed by a Napoleonic bureaucracy can now be released. The process of democratisation and decentralisation under way can make or break the future development of modern Spain and its participation on an equal footing in the scientific, technical and technological advances occurring elsewhere in the world.

The recent experience of other OECD countries shows that it is increasingly difficult, if not impossible, to control complex modern education systems from a single centre. The examiners consider that in Spain the new statutes and laws on regional autonomy represent a giant step in the direction of decentralisation. In particular, they would endorse the policy whereby the central government guarantees a minimum level of education across the nation, leaving each Autonomous Region to use whatever ends and means it chooses to build on the minimal foundations. If that equalising formula did not exist, the examiners would be concerned about the feasibility of upholding the equity principle across regions.

From what the examiners observed in four of the six Autonomous Regions (the Basque region, Galicia, Catalonia and Andalusia), the authorities are beginning to make independent decisions about the future development of education within their boundaries, especially as regards planning future requirements and teaching programmes and syllabuses. At the same time, it must be stressed that the degree of independent action varies even among these four regions. Most progress towards *full status* has been made in the Basque region and Catalonia, where almost all the central government powers have been transferred. Almost no progress towards independent decision-making appears to have been made, however, in the eleven regions which are to become partially or fully autonomous in the future.

Nevertheless, the ground-work for the necessary devolution is now in place. In the Basque region and Catalonia, the regional governments will soon also be responsible for higher, as well as school-level, education. In addition, they now have specific financial responsibilities. The Basque country collects taxes and remits the proceeds to the central government after deducting what is required for their own purposes, including the funds required for education. However, since the revenue remaining in the Regions corresponds to the former level of central government funding plus a percentage for the general rise in education spending at national level, no revolutionary change has really occurred.

The Basque region and Catalonia are levying their own additional taxes for education spending. While this is commendable, it will eventually pose problems for the overall relationship between the Regions and the central government. The examiners understand the government's hesitation to offend regional sensitivities at this early stage since the battle for overcoming major regional disparities in the development of education will be won or lost on the equity of public spending. But before long the Ministry of Education will probably have to propose a revised scheme for educational funding so as to prevent the decentralisation process from accentuating existing regional disparities instead of reducing them.

We do not propose to dwell on the detailed measures to promote the regionalisation and democratisation of education, including the creation of state school councils, the transfer of responsibility for capital expenditures, routine maintenance and payment of teaching staff to the Autonomous Regions, bilingual teaching in universities in the near future and establishment of joint transfer commissions. We do wish to argue, however, that the central government, and in particular the Ministry of Education and Science, will have to devise a *global scheme* for the future development of educational regionalisation in the form of a single system for *all the Autonomous Regions* and not just the first six, that is, prerogatives should not be attributed to Autonomous Regions on an individual basis. If the problem is not tackled across the board, there is a grave danger that rights and responsibilities will be hotly "disputed" and conflict with the central government will become endemic. Failure to work out such an overall formula could also have important political repercussions by arousing a sense of disillusionment in some of the Autonomous Regions and fanning separatist tendencies. It could also give rise to demands by traditionalist and conservative elements for a restoration of bureaucratic central control over the entire education system.

Early effects of decentralisation

Having struck that warning note, the examiners hasten to record that the fruits brought by decentralisation are already visible. In the Autonomous Regions that they visited comprehensive plans for the development of education have already been formulated. In the Basque region, for example, the main guidelines have been mapped out as follows:

   a) schooling to be conducted within a framework of Basque culture and values; in particular, the number of traditional Basque schools Ikastola will be increased;
   b) improvement of EGB provision, particularly in the upper forms (10-14 year-olds) and of the curriculum in addition to the basic nation-wide curriculum;
   c) acceleration of the specialised education programme;
   d) strengthening of higher education institutions and more open access to them for specialists who have hitherto been unable to attend courses at a Basque university;
   e) further democratisation of the Basque education system through the devolution of powers and responsibilities to local government bodies;
   f) initiation of talks with the central government on educational standards and financing at both Autonomous Region and national levels;
   g) improved training facilities for teaching staff who will teach in Basque and create the conditions required for genuinely bilingual education;
   h) confronting the issue of using textbooks in the Basque language. In the opinion of the proponents of a specifically Basque culture and bilingual education, new textbooks and teachers are required.

Andalusia, Catalonia and Galicia have established similar aims. The vivid impression left with the examiners after their all too brief visits to the Autonomous Regions was of a collective will to bring about change and to raise the overall quality of education. Present deficiencies were exposed with refreshing frankness as were the human and material limitations on accelerating the reform process. Decentralisation certainly appeared to have had a powerful tonic effect. The problem for the longer term is going to be how to sustain the initial mood of enthusiasm and zest for experiment and how to make sure that administrators and teachers at the municipal, district and small community levels are as much imbued with the spirit of innovation as senior officials in the administrative capitals.

One consequence of the devolution of powers from the centre is the need to build up what amounts to a ministry of education in each Autonomous Region, not to speak of education departments in towns and rural areas. That is no easy task. The centralised bureaucracy may have been, and indeed may still be, the butt of allegations about its lack of imagination, its top-heavy structure and its affection for red tape, but it did comprise a wealth of experience and professional expertise. Some officials will be moving from the centre to posts in the new ministries. There will still be a great shortage, however, of administrators and advisers competent to hold down senior positions. The examiners were impressed by the energy and enthusiasm of the officials they encountered in the Autonomous Regions. They wonder, however, whether sufficient care is being taken to train newly appointed officials, who are nearly all drawn from the ranks of school teachers, for their important responsibilities, and to monitor the effectiveness of their performance. Some courses for administrators are already arranged by the Ministry of Education. Will an adequate number of courses for educational administrators now be arranged throughout the country?

Throughout Spain, the examiners were struck by a feature of the terms of appointment of officials in public office that other countries might wish to contemplate if not emulate. This is an insistence on fixed-term appointments. Officials do not enjoy indefinite tenure. On the contrary, they are expected to serve as head of the education service, director of a department or as an inspector for a fixed term only. At the completion of that term they must return to the schools or to another post. Such a staffing policy is evidently democratic. It also means that there is constant mobility and very little of the mutual misunderstanding or even hostility that frequently divides administrators from teachers.

IV

BASIC GENERAL EDUCATION (EGB)

(Enseñanza General Básica)

Place of EGB in the education system

In Spain, basic general education (hereinafter designated EGB) in the strict sense of the term covers the period of compulsory schooling, which is currently 8 years, from age 6 to 14. Its present structure was laid down essentially in the General Education Act of 1970: a common school for all pupils between 6 and 14 years old divided since 1981 into three age groups: 6 to 8, 8 to 11, and 11 to 14 (i.e.: 2 + 3 + 3). The Spanish authorities are convinced that the whole school system needs to be reshaped and reformed, and important legislation has just been passed, namely, the LODE (*Ley Organica reguladora del Derecho a la Educación*) of 15 March 1984 [1]. In the strategy being developed at present, EGB plays a central role. All those interviewed by the examiners said they gave top priority, both in thought and in deed, to its reform. Afterwards, in order, comes the reform of pre-school education, education for 14 to 16 year-olds (*enseñanzas medias*) and upper secondary education. That list is illuminating. It reflects the major concern of the Spanish authorities to ensure adequate basic education for all, so as to raise the cultural level of the whole country, ensure real equality of opportunity in life, improve the results achieved at higher levels of education and strengthen democracy.

Although post-compulsory education must be diversified and may, it is acknowledged, necessitate some selection determined by individual aptitudes and intellectual merit, the aim of EGB is to *standardize results* rather than standardize opportunity. Selection on the ground of failure is therefore not acceptable at this level [2]. That aim explains the outlook adopted by the Spanish authorities and the strategy they are developing: everything possible must be done to eliminate failure. The role of basic education is to make up for social and individual inequalities and, what is more, avoid selection at too early an age [3]. Hence the priority given to developing and improving pre-school education, since proper instruction at this level constitutes an excellent, if not indispensable, preparation for primary school; hence, also, the calling into question of the 14-to-16 year-old cycle. There now seems to be agreement that compulsory schooling should be extended to age 16, but this extension will only be of benefit if the performance of pupils at EGB is markedly improved. This is an important point in the strategy for education and one which will be discussed again later. Meanwhile, increased attendance at the 14-16 level of education must be encouraged by a system of grants, and experiments are currently being conducted with a view to developing worthwhile upper secondary education of a technical nature which will make it possible to achieve a better balance between the numbers of students going into the two branches of education. In 1982, 400 000 pupils went from EGB into BUP (*Bachillerato Unificado Polivalente*) and 250 000 into FP (*Formación Profesional*). Fewer students enrol in FP than in university; in the first stage, enrolments in FP account for only 18 per cent of young people in the 14-to-15 age group (first stage) and 13 per cent of the second stage age group. The statistics show that 200 000 14-to-16 year-olds do not attend any educational establishment, although it is forbidden by law to work before the age of 16.

The authorities are convinced of the necessity of co-ordinating the 11-to-14 and 14-to-16 year-old cycles. How is this link to be formed? Several possibilities are envisaged which would involve retaining the present system with the break at age 14 or changing it and creating an intermediary cycle for 12-to-16 year-olds. The question seems still to be undecided. Clearly, the decision will affect the structure of EGB, as well as its position and role within the whole education system. Uncertainty on this point should not be allowed to continue for too long, otherwise the impetus of the reform will be arrested.

Pre-school education

The Spanish authorities believe that, in addition to its specific benefits – relations with peers, learning to practice personal hygiene, physical and mental development – pre-school education is an effective means of preventing failure at primary school in that it helps children to mature intellectually and emotionally. At the same time, the sharp increase in the number of working mothers in certain neighbourhoods has also led to a demand for more pre-school places.

Pre-school education covers four years from age 2 to 6, divided into two levels: 2 to 4 years (*escuela maternal*) and 4 to 6 years (*escuela de párvulos*). In the 2-to-4 year-old level schooling is also organised by the Ministry of Labour, the National Assistance Institute and enterprises.

The ultimate aim of the government is for all children aged between 4 and 6 to receive schooling. Under a development plan drawn up in 1982, it was decided to build premises to provide 116 000 new places. To date, 84 000 new places have been made available. Preparatory work is under way on an Act concerning the organisation of classes for 4-to-6 year-olds (*escuelas de párvulos*). In 1982-83, 11 per cent of the 2-to-4 year-old age group received pre-school education, the figure for the 4-to-6 year-old age group being 85 per cent as against 81 per cent in 1979-80.

We were told several times during our visits that it was impossible to satisfy all pre-school needs. Government policy is therefore in response to parental demand. It should be noted that a significant proportion of pupils attend private schools: 30 per cent for the 4-to-5 year-olds and 35 per cent for the 5-to-6 year-olds. 37 343 teachers were employed in pre-school education in 1982-83, 60 per cent in the public sector and 40 per cent in the private sector. The level of teachers' qualifications can cause some problems, and this point will be discussed in the chapter on teacher training. For the rest, given the general lack of physical resources and learning materials, the pre-school sector appears to be functioning satisfactorily.

Quality of basic education

The General Education Act of 1970 was the starting point for considerable development of compulsory education in Spain in both quantitative and qualitative terms. Before 1970, primary education covered six years only, from age 6 to 12, and at age 10 there was the possibility of selection for the *Bachillerato* stream. Basic education has now been extended to age 14 and made compulsory, the age for starting both the *Bachillerato* and vocational train-ing has been put back to 14 years, and teaching principles have been redefined and programmes reviewed. The fundamental pedagogical principle underlying practice is that of mixed ability classes. In the mid-70s, growing interest began to be shown in assessment, and a policy of continuous assessment was chosen.

The number of schools increased from 117 369 in 1970-71 to 175 635 in 1979-80 despite the fact that, during the same period, there was a policy of concentrating pupils from rural and mountain areas in regional schools. There was an increase in the number of pupils from 3 929 569 in 1970-71 to 5 606 000 in 1979-80. As for teachers, numbers increased from 139 616 to 205 550 during the same period.

It can be said that since 1974-75, there has been 100 per cent enrolment in the 6-to-14 age group. These increases were the result of successive development plans (1971, 1973, 1975, 1977 – Moncloa Agreements), plans which concerned not only school construction but also programmes, techniques, teaching methods, assessment and teacher training. However, some 400 000 school places are estimated to offer inadequate facilities, especially in those outer suburbs of the larger cities where the population has multiplied during the last decade or so.

Since 1970, compulsory education has been much criticised and also much discussed. In January 1981, a Royal Decree again restructured EGB, laid down new programmes, es-tablished new rules of assessment, took steps to ensure the provision of remedial teaching and defined the goals to be achieved.

Nevertheless, the two essential EGB problems for the present government remain: to ensure full school attendance and improve the quality of the education offered. The 1981 reform is criticised for having been too theoretical and over-ambitious, for having been adopted without thorough testing in practice, prepared in administrative offices and imposed in blanket fashion without consulting parents or teachers, and for having laid down require-ments that were unnecessarily prescriptive.

An evaluation of the results achieved as compared to the goals fixed has been under-taken in the first cycle (age 6 to 8), the evaluation being based on a sample of 9 000 pupils and supplemented by a survey of teachers' opinions. In the case of the middle cycle (age 8 to 11), an evaluation was carried out during the year 1984-85 and it allegedly showed that, paradoxically, the goals laid down are often seen as over-ambitious but that it can also happen that very simple goals are not being achieved. Overall, 60 per cent of pupils succeed in only 42 per cent of initial courses. Moreover, 20 per cent of pupils are one year or more behind in their schooling. Lastly, one-third of those leaving eighth year EGB do so without a diploma (*graduado escolar*),having obtained only a certificate of attendance (*certificado de escolaridad*), which entitles the holder to enrol in vocational training but not in the academic stream of upper secondary education. It has therefore been decided to reconsider the problem and study the changes to be made in the 1981 reform with regard to the first two cycles.

As to the third cycle, application of the 1981 reform has been suspended and a new project prepared which, since the 1984-85 school year, has been tried out in some 50 educa-tional establishments. Teams of volunteer teachers have been organised, and contact es-tablished at regional level with teachers' centres (CEPs) and Educational Sciences Institutes (ICEs). A standing commission has been entrusted with the task of co-ordinating project operations.

Reform – A new development model

The Spanish authorities have set themselves the goal of an 85 to 90 per cent success rate in basic education. This is an ambitious programme given the above-mentioned statistic of a low 42 per cent success rate in initial courses for 60 per cent of first-cycle pupils. The authorities affirm that it is necessary for reasons that are political (to ensure active participation by citizens in political life), economic (to promote growth) and social (to ensure equality of opportunity).

Two techniques will be used: a review of objectives, which will specify the minimum to be achieved by all pupils, and a different style of development. Ministry officials feel that for such an ambitious plan to succeed there must be personal involvement on the part of teachers, parents, university teachers and, in particular, educational institutes, local authorities and the social and economic community. This conviction is accompanied and strengthened by the consideration that every school must be rooted in its particular milieu, for reasons which are both educational – pupils must learn to situate themselves in their environment – and methodological – the immediate environment is an important pedagogic resource.

It was therefore decided to proceed on a trial basis and to involve as many actors as possible in the reform project. Proposals for changes are drawn up by groups of teachers, then discussed with experts, educationists, psychologists and other specialists, after which a basic document is prepared and distributed for comment to teachers and interested groups. Changes may be made on the basis of such comments, after which the proposals are implemented on an experimental period for one year, with application on a general scale planned for the following year. For the initial cycle of the EGB, this general application is planned for 1986-87. In the middle cycle, the evaluation results being available in 1985, the reform could therefore be implemented nation-wide in 1987-88.

But the reform is not just a question of programming. It will succeed only if it becomes the commitment of all. Such a commitment can be achieved through the system of consultation, experimentation and concerted action described above. It is predicated also on decentralisation to independent authorities, which should promote contact between the education system and the relevant economic and social setting, and on the reorganisation of school administration. The LODE includes a section on the administration of state schools which are to be managed by an elected school council, comprising teachers and parents, with the power to elect the principal. One of the controversial points in the LODE system for state-subsidised private education is known, moreover, to concern the question of intervention by teachers, parents and, possibly, pupils in the administration of private education establishments (see Chapter VI). Other examples in the same vein include the setting up of independently-run centres for teachers, financial support for groups of teachers responsible for retraining, and the reorganisation of pedagogic institutions, which will make it possible to modify the initial training received by teachers and to speed up and intensify in-service training.

It can be seen from the strategy envisaged that the success of the reform will depend on the ability of the authorities to co-ordinate a relatively wide range of factors. This will certainly require a delicate touch, the more so as it is also hoped to galvanize the system by encouraging initiatives at widely varying levels. Such initiatives must be co-ordinated and must complement one another. That will be possible only if all those concerned feel they are taking part in a collective, large-scale movement. The general aim appears to be to strengthen the links between the education system and Spanish society, more especially as concerns:

- the economic cnanges required and the restructuring of the economy;
- the social changes desired: equality, and the improvement of the social, scientific and professional expertise of the whole nation;
- the political changes desired: decentralisation and the strengthening of democracy.

Is it possible to achieve a broad consensus on this point so as, in particular, to ensure the vital factor which is the continuance of these projects? In this respect, and more particularly with regard to basic education, the government has drawn up a three-year plan. The period is short for a reform of this magnitude which involves the active and conscious participation of a large number of persons and institutions of very different types. Should it be longer, therefore, or is the risk of problems accumulating to be set against the loss of impetus that might arise from operating within a longer time-scale?

Compensatory education and rural schools

This imaginative and ambitious strategy to modernise and improve the quality of EGB is accompanied by a programme of compensatory education introduced in 1983 by means of a decree. As concerns basic education more particularly , it contains measures to make this minimum level of education available to everybody, by means of:

- literacy campaigns;
- organising courses for adults, especially those who were not able to obtain the *graduado escolar*;
- organising special courses of instruction for 14-to-16 year-olds who are not receiving upper secondary education;
- subsidising educational establishments in less-favoured areas, and thereby supporting specific measures for educational development.

A Directorate-General for Educational Advancement was created in 1985. Its role is to implement a coherent policy in the many fields requiring education measures outside, or in support of the official education system (see Chapter VI). Here our concern is with rural schools at the EGB level.

There is a strong desire to raise the quality of education in rural schools, some of which are extremely isolated. One of the main objects of the 1970 Education Act was to remove or at least reduce rural and urban disparities. Until scarcely two years ago the strategy was to consolidate rural schools as much as possible by closing the smaller ones and relying heavily on an extensive and expensive transport service to bring the pupils to school, the assumption being that this offered the best means of providing adequate resources. As a result, numerous schools disappeared. The new strategy is to maintain schools even in very small and remote villages for three powerful reasons. The first concerns the children's educational and affective development. "Bussing" is now seen as bad for them and boarding is to be used only as a last resort. The second reason is that the government is anxious to encourage villagers to stay where they are both to avoid rural depopulation and decay and to stop the flow of migrants into the towns and cities where there is already high unemployment. It is, of course, a familiar tale in many countries that parents often leave their villages when there is no nearby school for their children to attend. The third reason is that an increasing number of village parents object to sending their children to a distant school and insist upon having a school of their own. Thus, a plan is being implemented to bring about rural regeneration through joint action on the part of a number of ministries and a variety of regional agencies.

The new rural development strategy means, of course, that a considerable number of schools are still being staffed by a single teacher. A policy to overcome the one-teacher school problem, which is being tried out in a large number of areas, is to link together groups of villages in a network and to staff them by itinerant teachers based on a centrally located learning resource centre. The strategy necessitates the active co-operation and financial contribution of parents even if only in the form of unpaid labour. It also implies declining enrolments and consequential worries for the schools where the pupils had previously been concentrated. The Ministry of Education sets great store by this strategy and we ourselves were impressed by what we saw of two experiments, one in Valle del Amblès near Avila in Castille, and the other near Barcelona, two experiments among two hundred. In Valle del Amblès, six village centres are co-ordinated in a single network, one hundred and twenty pupils being taught by nine teachers. The teachers, most of them very young and carefully selected, move from one school to another. One of the teachers is a psychological guidance specialist, a second, a pedagogical specialist and a third, a specialist on learning disabilities. There is a learning resource centre from which teaching aids can be made available to each school as the timetable requires. The curriculum is taught in fifteen-day blocks of time. There is stress on individualising learning. Projects are selected to reflect the history and current character and problems of the local environment; nature studies figure prominently. Sports, theatre and music facilities are shared.

This experiment appears to work remarkably well. The teachers are visibly highly motivated and keen on testing new methods. The parents are no less enthusiastic. It was they, indeed, who adapted premises to create the schools and it is they who maintain them and who take turns to cook school meals. Teachers carry their materials with them and pupils buy their own books. Still, there is a shortage of resources which needs to be remedied, particularly as the experiment is relatively inexpensive and the existence of a school staffed by dynamic and *avant-garde* teachers is important for the cultural development of the whole community. The rural strategy adopted by Spain is relevant to the situation that prevails in many OECD countries and deserves to be widely known.

Special education

Children who are physically or mentally handicapped, and socially deprived or other special categories of children are taught in special schools or in special units within ordinary schools. The current trend is rather to bring handicapped children into the normal system. A decree is being prepared which provides for such integration over a period of eight years. At the same time, the various types of handicap, the materials needed and the training required by teachers will be specified.

A programme for detecting handicaps in children aged between 0 and 2 is being finalised. An experiment to be carried out in 1985-86 involves the introduction of two types of handicapped children into a centre serving a region with a population of 150 000. By the time the programme ends, there should be only 30 per cent of children remaining in special centres, the other 70 per cent attending ordinary centres.

Inspection

The inspection of EGB schools seems to be a source of some concern to the authorities. At present, the Inspectorate is an autonomous body responsible for its own recruiting. The proposal is to set up a system of recruitment based on aptitude tests and selection procedures. This is certainly a matter deserving attention.

The fact that responsibility for education is either divided between the central government and Autonomous Regions with, for example, elementary education on one side and other education on the other, or shared between them (for example, educational research, refresher courses for teachers and educational experiments) can give rise to complications. The role, structure, level of competence and functions of the inspectorate should therefore be re-examined in depth.

Teachers

A special chapter will be devoted to this topic, but attention should be drawn here to three points peculiar to EGB First, at present, there can be at least four types of teacher in a given school:

- those who attended a teacher training college before 1970 and received a non-specialised training;
- those who attended a university teacher training college after 1970, and received a specialised training;
- those who have a university degree plus a teaching certificate from an ICE;
- those who have a university teaching certificate.

There is even a fifth category comprising teachers who qualified before 1970 and then took a university correspondence course in a particular subject.

We were told that all teachers receive the same salary. However, it is obvious that problems of areas of competence and dividing lines can arise and that competition to teach the older classes can be keen. All this may have an adverse effect on team spirit, one of the cornerstones of the reform. More worrying, perhaps, is the fact that for the first five years, classes may be given to teachers trained to teach a particular subject and not well qualified to give general instruction in all subjects.

Secondly, there is the more general problem of co-ordinating education policy in schools with what teachers have been trained to teach. Clearly, the matter is complicated here, as elsewhere, by the fact that specialisation tends to imply upper secondary education and is therefore perceived as conferring more prestige and as likely to open the door to teaching at upper secondary level, or at least in the future 14 to 16 year-old cycle. This is a problem which we feel requires clarification.

Finally, all trainee teachers are at present "specialists" in the sense that the major part of their training (of three years following the *Bachillerato*) is in one of three specialised branches – sciences, the humanities, and linguistics – this training being completed by courses in psychology, pedagogy and teaching practice. Yet the current system is that for the first two EGB cycles (age 6 to 11) classes have just one teacher. Thereafter teachers take subjects in accordance with their specialisation.

We shall return to the whole question of the condition of teaching in Chapter VII.

NOTES AND REFERENCES

1. The entry into force of this Act has been suspended following an appeal challenging its constitutionality.
2. José Maria Maravall, *La reforma de la enseñanza, op.cit.*, p. 89.
3. *Ibid*, p. 87.

V

POST-COMPULSORY SECONDARY EDUCATION
(Enseñanzas Medias)

Reform plans

The Spanish term *enseñanzas medias* refers to that level of education immediately following compulsory schooling (EGB) and corresponds to what in other countries is designated the upper secondary cycle. Under the present law it is split into two branches: the BUP (*Bachillerato Unificado Polivalente*) plus COU (*Curso de Orientación Universitaria*), which is academic and prepares for the baccalaureate, and the first and second stages of vocational education and training FP (*Formación Profesional*). BUP is open to pupils with an EGB certificate.

The reform plans will change the structure of this cycle, since education will be made compulsory up to the age of 16 and the cycle for the 14-16 year-olds will be made comprehensive and provide a common trunk. It is probable that, if current intentions materialise, the succeeding cycle – 16-to-18 or 19 years – will be split into two branches: one, academic, leading to long-cycle university education and the other, vocational, leading to direct entry into working life and eventually, where desired, to short-cycle higher education. The plans for this second cycle of secondary education, which will then correspond to *post-compulsory* secondary education, are not yet clarified, at least in the minds of the examiners, though this is a topic of great interest to them, particularly at a time when many other OECD countries are faced with the challenge of how best to structure the upper secondary sector and to build effective bridges between general education and vocational education and training.

According to the Background Report prepared by the Spanish authorities: "the *Bachillerato*, as it stands at present, although observing the letter of the law (Decree of the 23rd January 1975), has to a large extent distorted the idea of a formative secondary education, which prepares people as much for life as for higher education" (p. 337). Although this is a criticism which could equally well be addressed to many systems of academic secondary education, it does raise the question whether the present plans for the reform of the 14-to-16 year-old cycle will indeed correct the distortion referred to, or whether the idea itself is really valid. To "prepare people for life" is, at the least, an ambiguous aspiration, and to "prepare for higher education" is a goal about which no agreement can be reached among the several actors involved. As to COU, the prevalent conviction among the teachers whom we met, endorsed by the Background Report, is that it is yet one more year of the *Bachillerato* with the addition of a moderate selective function for university entrance. We heard radical condemnations of it as being "useless" since it would offer neither a better preparation to the students, nor more efficient guidance in the sensible choice of a career, nor even an effective screening instrument. The high rate of failure in the first university year would seem to support this radical criticism, if only partially, but other reasons can be adduced for the lack of effectiveness of the system and the Background Report itself discusses them in detail.

Our own purpose here, however, is to stress the need for viewing the system as a whole, for defining the structure and contents of *all* the various cycles and for avoiding gaps between cycles. As to the criticisms above, some pertinent questions may have to be asked such as: Is the present first university year appropriate in terms of its content, its pedagogic adequacy and its functional relevance? Or does it, at least in some cases, consist of too much ornamental knowledge, such as abstract physics and mathematics or, indeed, other subjects of doubtful utility which are detrimental to the creativity, interest and application of the students? Not many university professors will acknowledge the need to reconsider the content and methods of university studies but when one speaks of "preparing for higher education" it is necessary to be clear-sighted as to objectives and to seek the best ways and means of achieving them.

The same can be said about the meaning of "to prepare for life". Is it just a question of teaching towards an occupation and skills which the student leaving the education system may or may not actually use, or does it entail far more than that in striving to bring about the intellectual, cultural, affective, civic and physical development so vigorously argued for by educators? Needless to state, these problems are not specific to the Spanish education system, but since that system is undergoing sweeping reforms, which can only be justified in the cause of better quality and teaching effectiveness, it is important to know exactly what obstacles must be surmounted.

The same line of reasoning can be applied to vocational and technical education within the formal education system. This branch of secondary education is divided, as mentioned above, into two consecutive stages: FP1 (2 years) and FP2 (2 or 3 years); a third cycle FP3 was envisaged but has not so far been created. The primary objective is to train pupils for a specific occupation while simultaneously offering them a general education. Under the terms of the 1970 General Law of Education, the sector should maintain, in its organisation and functioning, a close relationship with the world of work, in continuance of the previous forms of vocational education that were initiated in the 19th century.

We understand that in certain communities there is a close relationship between the vocational schools and the world of work and that the majority of those who complete their courses find jobs nearby relatively easy. This was certainly true of one small community in Catalonia that we visited. In the main, however, the results are not commensurate with expectations: "the bridge that was envisaged between the education system and the production systems has never really happened, except in a very few cases" (Background Report, p. 391), and this vocational branch of education is regarded by society as a second best choice or poor relation. Established as late as 1976, it lacks adequate resources and in many places it is popular neither with pupils nor parents, who equate it with failure. Worse, employers have little regard for the qualifications obtained in FP1, which carry little credit on the labour market, and prefer to take on young people without previous training in the education system. This blunt reality was revealed in recent enquiries by the Ministry of Labour and the University of Murcia and reaffirmed to the examiners by representatives of the employers' associations, CEOE and CEPIME.

The reasons for this harsh assessment are varied, but one of them is related to the intrinsic quality of the students who attend FP courses. The majority of these (80 per cent) fulfilled the attendance requirements in compulsory schooling but did not complete their courses and were granted no more than a certificate of attendance (*certificado de escolaridad*). Some of them have repeated up to two years in EGB; others have come from the

34

former *bachillerato elemental*, with only four years of schooling, and still others over 14 have had no previous school diploma, and were admitted by passing a simple entrance test. In these circumstances it is scarcely surprising that only about 40 per cent of the total number of pupils in FP1 finish this stage in two years and that some 35 per cent give up studying altogether and leave without a qualification, in addition to those who did not enter FP or BUP at all, a total estimated at over 300 000 youngsters aged 13-16. Thus, it is not just a question of the "relevance" of the training offered – even if this be an important factor – but of improving the general "quality" of the output of FP1.

Similar arguments apply to FP2, which is taken up by only about 20 per cent of the total number of pupils who have left BUP with or without graduation (most of them without it), of which about 38 per cent drop out (26 per cent in the third-year course). It is manifestly an uneconomic operation and represents a considerable waste of human resources, which must be reconsidered when plans for the reform of the upper secondary cycle are finally drawn up.

Other problems still remain. One is the large number of programmes accessible in FP (the figure of 56 was quoted to us) of which two absorb a majority of students: Administration (34.8 per cent) and Electricity and Electronics (23.2 per cent). Most courses elicit minuscule demand and some appear to be virtually obsolescent.

This, again, is a question which deserves thorough investigation if all these or similar programmes are to be maintained after the reform. Even more disturbing is the fact, quoted in the Background Report, that most of the graduates obtain jobs requiring skills different from those that they have struggled to master at school. The acquired knowledge is, consequently, almost useless, and the objective of preparing for working life is thereby thwarted.

Labour market inquiries have indicated that the best posts and salaries have been obtained by young people trained on the job (80 per cent of the total). This suggests that it is more beneficial for students to abandon studies and take up employment wherever they can find it. The type of qualification obtained is related to salaries only in the case of technical or managerial level jobs, and not at all for semi-qualified administrative staff, skilled or semi-skilled workers. Enquiries addressed to companies have also revealed that, for 74 per cent of workers recruited by industry, all that was required by employers was some basic education, except for managers, executives and heads of department, for whom a university degree was normally required (72 per cent of examples). Even foremen today have usually experienced short-cycle higher education, whereas such posts were filled in the past by those who had passed through the old industrial FP. The conclusion to be derived from these various observations is that the present FP is not much appreciated. Indeed, we were informed that employers believe that it is neither useful nor necessary. All this evidence points to the conclusion that a carefully conceived alternative scheme is required before embarking on the creation of a new separate branch of vocational training at the level of upper secondary education.

In any case, there is a general progressive trend among employers according to which FP courses ought not to be taught as a kind of limited apprenticeship for a specific trade or job, but rather as many-sided, directed to modern and emerging occupational requirements and flexible changes of jobs and reconversions. The more traditional occupations and skills may well be prepared for outside the education sector, under the auspices of the Ministry of Labour or, preferably, through concerted schemes with enterprises and services. The implications of these views will be further discussed below.

Resources and effective outcomes

The financing of secondary education poses a formidable problem. In 1982 there was a deficit of 220 000 places and a plan to provide for 155 000 new ones. Before discussing in more detail the present reform projects, we feel it necessary, therefore, to offer some reflections on available resources and the effectiveness of the system. The data provided in the Background Report show that academic upper secondary education is carried out in public and private establishments, the latter being in the majority (55 per cent). However, the number of teachers does not parallel the number of schools, since 63 per cent of teachers are employed in public institutions. The disparity is explained when account has been taken of the total of class contact hours, which is higher for private schools, and of the contractual obligations of the teachers (94 per cent full-time and over for public schools, as compared with 34 per cent only for private schools). Thus, in public schools teachers are required to be present in the school outside class contact hours and may also be required to assume administrative and other duties, whereas in private schools teachers are usually present in school only for the hours they actually teach. Since the number of students in public schools is also considerably higher (66 per cent compared with 34 per cent in private schools), the student/class and student/teacher ratios are not substantially different in public and private institutions.

The situation is similar in FP although the figures vary slightly (42 per cent of the schools are public, with 59 per cent of the teachers and 55.7 per cent of the students). The majority of BUP teachers are graduates in arts (about 50 per cent) and sciences (about 30 per cent) and a few have doctorates. About 17 per cent in public schools and 26 per cent in private schools are not graduates, usually teachers of religion or artistic subjects.

Teachers in the academic schools have limited pedagogical training, and little in-service training is provided. There are also examples of a lack of correlation between the academic degree obtained and the subjects actually taught owing to a variety of reasons fully explained in the Background Report. At the same time, the teachers in the BUP schools we visited were manifestly enthusiastic about their work. Mostly young, they reported no disciplinary problems but, on the contrary, excellent relations with their pupils. They tended to complain, however, that the curriculum was overloaded, that there were too many hours in the school day and that there were too many pupils per class to permit proper attention to individual needs and problems. They also lamented their own lack of pedagogical training and the limited opportunity for in-service training. The obvious need for corrective measures and for improvement in teacher training activities is acknowledged by the Spanish authorities and considered by us in Chapter VII.

Teachers in the vocational schools, with rare exceptions, have little or no training in pedagogics. Those "teaching" practical subjects have relevant practical experience but no training in educational theory and instructional methods. We were struck, however, by the youth and enthusiasm of the teachers whom we met and by the good university qualifications of those responsible for academic subjects.

At a rough estimate, 30 per cent of the BUP schools are considered to be performing well and 40 per cent adequately; the remaining 30 per cent are considered to be either relatively or extremely deficient. Again, there are no corresponding data for FP schools, but to judge from the sample we visited, some are quite good and well equipped, whereas others lack adequate facilities and equipment, especially laboratories and workshops. As stated in the Background Report: "There is a lack of proportion between space in classrooms, laboratories, workshops and special classrooms" (pp. 405-406). A particular effort will be necessary to train and stimulate teachers to use the equipment available for practical classes. We saw for ourselves in one or two schools some excellent equipment in mint condition simply because it had never been used.

As to the effectiveness of the system, it is recognised that it gives reasons for concern. We have already commented on the situation in FP where the figures for failures during the period 1981-83 are over 62 per cent. They are also high for BUP, that is, of the order of 50 per cent at the end of the cycle. The average repeating rate is about 19 per cent in public schools and 8 per cent in private schools, a fact that seems to militate in favour of the quality of the private institutions, since the figures for COU, corresponding to national examinations, are close to those given above. Needless to say, the students in private institutions come, on average, from more privileged social backgrounds and this largely explains their higher academic achievement.

A final point worth noting is the inequality between regions. Rates of schooling obviously vary according to demographic distribution and other factors. The national average is about 30 students per 1 000 inhabitants. Madrid and the Basque region are above this average. Andalucia, Valencia, La Rioja and Catalonia are below the average and Extramadura, Baleares, and Castilla-la-Mancha have the lowest figures at about 24-25 students per 1 000 inhabitants. In order to encourage greater participation in upper secondary education the government has adopted a policy of granting scholarships. The examiners were not apprised of other studies about the disparities as reflected in rates of achievement and drop-outs, which might yield interesting information and point to possible corrective measures. The widely different economic potential of the various regions may lead to more pronounced disparities in the future given the difficult negotiations over the allocation of resources to the autonomous governments. A strong spirit of national solidarity will be necessary to avoid the widening of inequalities or their perpetuation.

Reform of secondary education

As commented above, the main outcome of the reform under experimental trial at this level of education will be the creation of a unified, comprehensive and compulsory two-year cycle, following EGB and replacing the first two years of BUP and FP1. This is considered to be in line with the trend throughout the western world to extend the period of compulsory education to a ten-year cycle in the cause of equality and of raising the overall stock of knowledge and skills in the population. At the same time, the content will be modernised and adapted to the present era of constant innovation and changing economic and social demands. The teaching-learning relationship will be modified, with emphasis being put on a more active role for the individual learner, and the curriculum will shed its excess burden of stale knowledge.

The new cycle is intended to complete the education of the young person so that he or she can face the future as a worker and a citizen by avoiding premature choices of careers and acquiring, through closer contact with the surrounding environment, the capacity to make rational decisions. The plan of studies has been organised in pursuit of these objectives and in an attempt to complement the traditional subjects with experimental and social sciences, technology and the arts, these three latter occupying 30 per cent of the total timetable.

After this cycle the intention appears to be to create a dual system with an academic COU-type cycle preparing for entrance to the long-cycle courses of the university and a FP cycle (2-3 years) preparing for an occupation or access to short-cycle university-level courses. These features of the reform are not documented in the Background Report.

The constraints lying in wait for the reform, especially the strengthening of vocational education and training, are formidable. They include: the structures and traditions of the teaching and learning process; entrenched habits and customs; the attitudes and training backgrounds of the principal actors (teachers, inspectors and parents); budgetary factors (buildings and equipment); public opinion. The debate on general and vocational education cannot be avoided and needs to be exhaustively conducted. No matter how well-intentioned and fundamental its purposes, the success of the reform will depend on a number of factors which cannot be anticipated at the present stage. Continuous evaluation of the experimental programmes will therefore be required in order to obtain essential information, mostly on the degree to which students accept the new approaches and on their comparative achievement. But these programmes will not easily be replicated throughout the system. They are being conducted by highly-motivated and well-prepared teachers, which will not always be the case when the experimental phase yields to general adoption. Many mistakes have been committed in the past, in Spain as elsewhere, owing to neglect of this important difference, the most noteworthy perhaps having recently concerned the teaching of "modern mathematics"; many of the teachers called upon to adopt this new method simply did not know how to cope and the results were accordingly disappointing.

Adequate preparation of teachers, not only in the pedagogical domain but as regards motivation, classroom management and cooperation with colleagues, is the fundamental prerequisite for any reform or, indeed, for any movement designed to raise the quality of education. The evidence and the data presented in the Background Report lead one to believe that the reorientation of teachers should be a high priority, all the more so since new active methods are envisaged.

Revision of programmes and content is also essential in order to correct the tendency towards over-specialisation and the teaching of "fashionable" subjects as opposed to subjects relevant to modern requirements. Several countries which were pioneers in adopting new curricula and apparently sound new methods are now confronted with grave educational problems.

As to the content of the future 2-year unified cycle, some concern was expressed to us about the possible lowering of minimum requirements, leading to a dilution of BUP standards. It is paradoxical that this tendency coexists with the transfer of certain subjects that require a high degree of sophistication and reasoning from the universities to the secondary level. The results may well be quite different from those expected if the two opposing tendencies are not reconciled, if vertical as well as horizontal co-ordination is not ensured and if teachers do not receive adequate training for the new roles they are expected to perform.

There is no guarantee that the new cycle will represent an improvement. It simply *looks* better on paper, and to replace FP1 by a cycle which will give the students a richer general background is a step in the right direction, particularly if the technological and arts component is treated as an integral and essential part of the curriculum and if good facilities and equipment are made available. However, the next stage should be clearly defined. The plan for a dual system is questionable since it will mean postponing to a later stage career choices which will have been socially biased from the start.

A diversified 2- or 3-year cycle with a strong vocational emphasis in the different subject areas regarded as of equal value and affecting equal possibilities of access to university courses is an alternative worth exploring, given that it is more in line with the general feelings and attitudes of employers and the characteristics of the labour market in the short-term perspective. Indeed, it is hard to think of a typical FP-type cycle of 2-3 years within the education system which could overcome the objections met by the present FP1 and FP2, even if addressed to more modern sectors of activity. On the other hand, there is no reason why a more humanist or technological cycle placed at the same educational level should be different in developmental capacity or social value, as there is no obvious justification for not having, in each of them, a strong vocational orientation, qualifying for entering the labour market if studies are not continued. The organisation of university courses in three cycles will also tend to reduce the barriers that continue to exist between short- and long- cycle courses and between the institutions in which they are offered.

Various models exist for the comprehensive upper secondary cycle of studies in terms of organisation, and there is now enough information for the content to be designed in adequate terms. It is clear from the results of enquiries and research that the courses taught at present in FP1 and FP2 do not correspond to the current or future needs of the labour market. Indeed, there is a definite decline in demand, as pointed out in a recent publication of the Ministry of Labour (*Requerimientos de empleo y formación profesional*).

These are times of flux and Spain is seeking technological innovation which requires a higher degree of professional mobility and an increased adaptability of workers to different jobs or tasks. The education authorities, employers and workers seem to be well aware of the consequences. At meetings with a variety of interlocutors, the examiners encountered a wide measure of consensus about the new demands on the education system imposed by the economic development of Spain, for example, the need for all pupils to learn how to identify, to define and to solve problems. It is unquestionable that this development will be achieved by means of increased productivity, implying that the *quantity* and *quality* of the labour force required will be different – better jobs will be available, but higher qualifications will also be required. The unanimous desire was for more general, less specialised, and more broadly-based vocational courses at the post-compulsory level, for example for the type of comprehensive school referred to above.

The document issued by the Ministry of Labour also identifies the main areas in which a need for training is anticipated: computer technology, automation, computer science, telecommunications, electronics, aquaculture, marine sciences, biotechnology, alternative energy sources and new materials are examples of new technological subjects, as administration and foreign languages are examples of the human and social sciences. The levels at which training is required in these and several other modern subjects are extensively examined in this document, which affords a solid basis for discussion between the education and labour authorities.

A final remark is perhaps in order on the need for co-ordinating horizontal policies at the political and operational levels. This is particularly true as far as labour and education policies are concerned, especially when, as now, the rate of youth unemployment is so high. Professional and vocational training programmes are conducted by the two Ministries and also by employers, but there does not appear to be a co-ordinated effort and a clear distinction of functions and objectives. Each Ministry and agency has its own specific field of activity. All aspects of vocational and professional training are complementary and applicable to concrete situations. The establishment of appropriate joint co-ordinating structures at the operational level, involving trade unions and employers associations, and of high-level policy-making units might be advisable measures to avoid the generation of divisive interests and competences in this critical area with a consequent waste of human, physical and financial resources. We are aware of the existence of a Coordinating Board of Vocational Training to advise the Ministry of Education, but this does not seem to us sufficiently representative of non-formal as well as formal educational interests.

VI

SPECIFIC ISSUES

Compensatory education

Equality of opportunity and, to the greatest possible extent, outcomes is, as we have seen, one of the major objectives of the authorities. Thus, one of the three "global objectives" of education is specified as "economic and social quality". As to application of the principle of equal opportunity "it has been observed that the quantity and quality of the services a person receives depend on his economic capacity, social level and place of residence. In order to break the vicious circle of the reproduction of inequality, the State has attempted to implement a compensatory education policy, integrating the citizens regardless of their social-economic, cultural and ideological differences"[1].

As pointed out in Chapter IV, the Minister of Education has established a Directorate-General for Educational Advancement, with a sub-directorate for compensatory education, in order to cater for the educational needs of all age groups. This is a bold initiative. Several countries have long had directorates for adult education within national ministries of education but there is no parallel among OECD countries for placing under a single directorate with, theoretically, the same status as any other directorate, responsibility for all the disadvantaged groups in the population whether children or adults. It will be interesting to see whether the Directorate can make its weight fully felt alongside the long-established and powerful directorates for basic and upper secondary education. Will there not be boundary disputes and will it command resources commensurate with the magnitude of its task? The examiners would also like to raise the issue of compensatory education in the Autonomous Regions. Will measures be taken to ensure that resources are equitably distributed so that areas suffering the greatest deprivation receive adequate financial support?

Language teaching

There are two kinds of language problems facing the schools in Spain: the first, which applies nation-wide, concerns the choice of a foreign language – essentially English or French – in the curriculum; the second, which applies only in regions cited in Chapter I, concerns teaching in their own language.

As to the first, it is the consequence of passing within the last decade from the domination of French language and literature to the domination of English in the curriculum. In EGB from the sixth year pupils spend three hours a week on a compulsory foreign language; almost half still study French. At the secondary level, however, English is overwhelmingly the first choice. Apart from other considerations this raises the problem of how to employ the large army of French specialists. The examiners visited one upper secondary school where the parent representatives complained that their children were obliged to learn French when nearly all of them wished to learn English. The examiners suggest that an inquiry into the teaching of modern languages should be instituted with a view to establishing the scale of demand for alternative modern languages and its implications for the recruitment and training of modern languages teachers in the future and, perhaps, retraining of some of the present teachers.

As to the second, it is ineluctable but it places a heavy burden on the curriculum and adds to educational costs. In Catalonia, for example, pupils are taught in Catalan but must also know Castilian Spanish as well as learning a foreign language. Many practical problems arise: adjustment of the timetable; supply of competent teachers; mixing of pupils with different first languages; need for new textbooks and specialised materials. The problems differ also between and within regions. Several OECD countries have long been accustomed to providing instruction in several languages, Yugoslavia being a striking example. The Spanish authorities might find it useful to discuss the curricular, pedagogical and financial problems that arise, and possible solutions, with other interested countries.

Arts and crafts

Vocational education and training in arts and crafts is a separate branch of education carried out in special schools. It was last regulated by specific legislation in 1963 and since then only minor adjustments have been made. Even the Education Law did not treat it according to its own merits and the present situation is rather ambiguous for lack of definition of future goals. The Background Report of the Spanish authorities makes no mention of it despite the world-famous cultural and artistic traditions of Spain which would seem to justify a special interest in the preservation of artists and craftsmen.

Still, there is no lack of demand; over 30 000 students are registered in official institutions (Music Schools and Schools of Applied Arts) and a further 100 000 undergo some kind of artistic training in private institutions or with the help of individual teachers. Many of these correspond to spare-time cultural or occupational activities but it is very likely that, if appropriate institutions were to be given adequate status, integrated into the official scheme of formal education at the upper secondary level and granted access to corresponding higher education courses – music, dramatic art and related professions, fine arts, architecture, design, etc. – an important percentage of students would be attracted to them and many potential talents would not be wasted.

To a certain extent, the situation today is not unlike that pertaining at the beginning of the century when many schools of applied arts were created throughout Europe to promote innovative design and provide a creative occupation for the leisure-time of workers. Some of these schools are thought to be out-dated and under-resourced but a reappraisal of their role would seem timely. This would imply separation of the cultural and professional training within each establishment and possible insertion of the professional ones within the structure of the upper secondary cycle, similar to other professional training courses. Optional arts subjects could also be added to the curriculum of basic education schools to provide alternative choices for the pupils with a definite artistic vocation. The recent Law on the Public Function paved the way for this insertion by equalising the levels of the teachers of the Schools of Applied Arts and of secondary schools, which, again, can attract qualified staff to those schools and avoid duplication of teachers of general subjects.

Although recognisably difficult and delicate in many aspects, the reform of vocational education and training in the arts deserves the attention and care of the Spanish authorities.

41

It would be regrettable if, within the framework of ambitious and would-be all-embracing educational reforms, an area so vital for preserving and strengthening Spain's rich cultural heritage should be neglected.

Private education

A large percentage of education in Spain is private; some 50 per cent of pre-school centres, 30 per cent of primary schools and 50 per cent of secondary schools; in total, 40 per cent of primary and lower secondary enrolments combined. Most of the private schools are located in the towns and cities. In Barcelona, for example, no fewer than 50 per cent of pupils are attending them.

Since 1972 the government has subsidised the private schools. As in Denmark no less than 85 per cent of each school's expenditure, assessed according to the total of pupil enrolments, is financed by the State. The assumption underlying this generous rate is that fees can be kept down to a reasonably low level so that no parents will be deterred from sending their children to a private school because of the prohibitive cost. It is also fully recognized that, apart from the principle of freedom of choice for parents, there is no way for the foreseeable future in which the State could satisfy the huge demand for places at all levels.

At the same time, the State is intent upon raising the quality and increasing the places in the public system with the long-term expectation that the demand for privately-provided education will diminish. The Law on the Right to Education (LODE) also prescribes regulations according to which private schools shall operate. They must, for example, offer open access and maintain minimum standards of instruction and buildings and equipment.

It must be stressed that the functions and status of private schools cannot crudely be compared with those obtaining in countries where private education exists for an elite or for predominantly religious purposes. Many of them, in Barcelona for example, were set up in opposition to the ill-regarded public schools under the Franco regime. Some are very poor. A few are elite establishments. All would claim to be performing a vital social service and all would affirm that in a democratic State parents should have the right to choose schools for their children that reflect their own values or religious beliefs.

Until as recently as the month of November 1984 there were no signs impending of any serious public controversy over the present and future role of private schools. Since then, however, there has been a good deal of opposition from private school interest groups to what is regarded as the government's new tendentious policies.

Private schools follow the same curriculum as the public schools. Their teachers, however, are appointed by each school's governing board and are thus less well protected in terms of tenure and working conditions than their public counterparts with their status of civil servants. They are also less well remunerated and, as a rule, teach longer – often considerably longer – hours. This may be regarded as the price to be paid for freedom of choice but it does raise two important issues.

One issue is over the question of the control and management of all schools, whether they be public or private. The official policy is to seek democratisation through teachers in a given school working as a team and the greater participation of parents. It is difficult to see how this policy can be implemented in those private schools where the teachers have traditionally had insecure tenure and no role in determining school objectives, and where there appears to be reluctance to bring about effective parent participation. The LODE is designed to rectify this situation and the question is whether its prescriptions will prove effective.

A second issue is concerned with equity. A private school having received 85 per cent of its costs from the State can then proceed to raise additional revenue from fees, though ceilings are set by the LODE. Moreover, it can expect many parents to spend considerable sums on such things for their children as school uniforms, books, and musical instruments. In other words, children in private schools, heavily subsidised by the State, may well be much better served in terms of "extras" than pupils in the state schools. There are, of course, some public schools in well-to-do neighbourhoods where pupils also enjoy special privileges thanks to the expenditures of their parents.

Adult education

To expand and enrich the provision of adult education is declared to be a high priority of the present administration. It is swayed by three main considerations: i) a concern for social justice; thus, adults who did not receive or could not complete their basic education are entitled to make good their educational deficiencies; ii) the need for well-informed and active citizens to help consolidate the establishment of democratic institutions and practices; iii) the need for a better skilled and more adaptable adult working population.

The difficulty is how to mount a nation-wide, full-scale effort on behalf of adult education while simultaneously confronting the consequences of the massive expansion of education for children and young adults. The enthusiasm and will to succeed are undoubtedly there and, as we have stressed, the authorities have set up a fully-fledged sub-directorate to deal with compensatory education, of which adult education is seen as an integral part and a high priority. Nor is there any lack of indicative planning. In June 1984 the Ministry of Education published a White Paper on The Education of Adults which comprises a historical and descriptive account of the field, valuable statistics about adults with learning needs, and a detailed strategic and organisational plan of action. The critical question remains: how can the aspirations expressed in the White Paper be translated into reality? For their part, the examiners are convinced that little progress can be made without greatly increased resources and more effective use of existing capacity.

For those studying to complete their basic education special centres have been set up. We were informed that in general these are located in old buildings and operate with limited resources. A centre that we visited in Madrid, however, had been purpose-built, and though by no means luxurious, it was adequately equipped. The centres have two main functions: to fill the gap in the education of those who left school without a certificate and to offer opportunities for some specialisation, for example, secretarial work. It would be desirable to undertake an inventory of needs in order to cover all communities, and meet the needs of all those who seek learning opportunities. The centres are not likely to touch, however, those who do not wish to return to "school" or who are allergic to all organised forms of education.

A system of correspondence education at the non-university level, organised in modules, has also been established. Two national centres provide courses for EGB and BUP, respectively: the National Institute of Basic Education by Correspondence and the National Centre of Teaching of Baccalaureate by Correspondence. Both centres supplement correspondence courses by arranging for students to meet teachers at centres located throughout the country. There is a proposal, which seems to us highly desirable, to inaugurate correspondence courses in vocational training, particularly for those subjects that do not require expensive practical equipment.

We had little time to visit adult education centres outside Madrid, to speak with professional adult educators or to inquire closely into the provision of adult education at the community level. Nevertheless, we have arrived at some tentative conclusions that may merit consideration.

In the first place, we gained the impression that the teaching courses and materials as well as the methods in use are somewhat rigid and traditional. Adults undoubtedly can learn more effectively when content, materials and methods are designed with their characteristics in mind rather than those of children and young people. What are the prospects for creating many more *purpose-designed* adult education centres?

Secondly, we wonder if all the potential resources in each community are being adequately harnessed. Are local surveys of needs taking place? Are efforts being made to identify and exploit all the available human resources and all the available funds and accommodation?

Thirdly, we suspect that there is a lack of programme articulation between and across the various agencies concerned directly or indirectly with the needs of adults. Is there not a case for setting up a planning and coordinating committee in each local area?

Fourthly, we suspect, once again, that there is a lack of articulation of policies and financing between and across ministries at the national level. Is there a need for a national advisory or consultative board on adult education, comprising representatives of all the government organs and major non-governmental agencies concerned with adult education?

Fifthly, there appears to be a lack of professionalism in the field of adult education, associated with the absence of applied research inquiries into adult learning needs and problems. We would suggest that centres for training adult educators should be set up in the universities or elsewhere, centres which might also begin to develop a research capacity.

Finally, we wonder whether it would not be desirable to appoint a broadly-based national commission to inquire into the adequacy of the existing provision for adult education and to recommend ways and means of improving it. The White Paper would provide an excellent point of departure for the deliberations of such a commission.

School children abroad

As explained in Chapter I, 60 000 young Spanish people of school age are living abroad. The Ministry of Education has established a network of centres abroad to permit young people and adults to follow the same curricula at the several levels of education as in Spain. The examiners have no comment to make on this area of concern except to say that for Spain, as for the other OECD Mediterranean countries, it is obviously vital to ensure that the children of emigrants do not lose their sense of national identity and their distinctive Spanish culture. To that end it is hoped that Spain will continue actively to support such intergovernmental activities as that on Education and Cultural and Linguistic Pluralism currently taking place under the CERI programme of OECD.

Role of parents

As pointed out in Chapter I, the Spanish family remains a much stronger unit than in most OECD countries, with beneficial consequences for children's schooling. Most parents are deeply devoted to their children's education. They are willing to pay for many of the extras – books, pens, paper and so on – that the financially overstretched public system cannot supply, and to organise fund-raising ventures. Moreover, as illustrated above, many are prepared to contribute to the maintenance of private schools. At the same time, most parents appear to be content to leave education to professional educators. They assume that education is a good thing. A few of the principals and teachers whom we interviewed wryly informed us that many parents also expected too much of their children's schools.

The examiners can only endorse, however, the public policy to encourage parents to become more directly involved in the daily life of the schools. The law specifies that "there may be parents' associations" in each school and that they "may utilise the premises of the teaching establishments in order to carry out their activities, so that the principals shall facilitate the integration of said activities in the scholastic course, always bearing in mind the development of the latter". The challenge is how to ensure that parents' associations are formed in each school and that they shall play an active role rather than one largely determined by the principal and teachers. Closer relations between class teachers and parents might help to create groups of involved parents. The examiners would also recommend the institution of courses for parents designed not only to inform them about the development problems and learning needs of their children but also how to form and manage effective associations.

NOTE

1. *España: Desarrollo de la educación en 1981-83, op. cit.,* p. 391.

VII

TEACHERS AND THEIR TRAINING

Training facilities

The great majority of teachers in the public schools in Spain are civil servants with the right to remain in post until the age of 65; a minority are employed under contract. Many do not belong to any kind of trade union, particularly those employed in private schools. Unions, in any case, only came into existence some six years ago. In 1984 the number of teaching associations and salary scales in the public service was reduced from over thirty to four, that is, one general corps and one scale for each primary and secondary level. Nevertheless, conflicts of status and special interests persist.

Traditionally, teachers destined for the compulsory school and pre-school level were trained in colleges, pre-school teachers and teachers of handicapped children receiving additional special training. Since 1972 the colleges have been incorporated in University Schools of Training of Teachers of General Basic Education. The universities continue, however, to regard them as inferior places of learning.

As far as we could ascertain there has been little positive change in their aims, internal organisation and methods, though the change has enabled the staff to teach fewer hours for higher salaries. There seems to have been no impact on the nature of the courses offered; there is no interaction with university faculties and teachers; the colleges do not have a research function. One college visited by us was physically located at some considerable distance away from its parent university, thereby reinforcing its sense of isolation. New recruits to teaching posts in the colleges must have a PhD. Many of the existing staff, however, have minimal academic qualifications. Moreover, there is very little in-service training available to them. As in some other countries, there is accordingly the problem of how to train the trainers.

The main weakness in initial training appears to lie in the lack of a strong component of educational theory and practice. Students are trained essentially as academic specialists in discrete subjects rather than as pedagogues. It is evident that the new reforms will call for a great effort on the part of teachers to cope with new syllabuses and integrated subjects and to change their attitudes, styles and methods. For some, indeed, it will mean assuming new roles.

In-service training is particularly weak, partly because of the sheer shortage of programmes and partly because of the difficulty many teachers experience in obtaining leave from their regular duties in order to attend courses. Some do attend evening and summer courses, however, though on a voluntary basis. It is especially difficult to find qualified trainers for conducting in-service courses.

Teachers in the secondary schools hold degrees (at least the licentiat which requires five years) in one or more subjects but have virtually no training in educational theory and practice. Recruitment and promotion are determined by success in competitive examinations (*oposiciones*) rather than proven performance as a teacher *per se*. Opportunities for in-service training are few and far between.

Principals receive no specific training for the administrative and managerial tasks they are required to perform. The question of a valid career structure is now being considered.

The authorities at the national Ministry of Education and in the regions are anxious to raise the level of teaching effectiveness. They are aware of the present deficiencies in the initial and in-service training arrangements and in the rewards and incentives on offer. Our comments are designed to contribute some ideas on the future of teacher policies.

Reform projects

In 1982, a working party was officially set up to study the reform of teacher training centres. It has submitted its conclusions, but these have not yet been implemented. In 1984, however, the Ministry of Education and Science published a draft plan for the reform of initial and in-service training, which strongly criticised the present situation and proposed radical changes. Every teacher should be required to follow interdisciplinary studies at university level and the EGB colleges should be dissolved.

As for the training of upper-secondary education teachers, pedagogical training suffers, as indicated in the Background Report, from a lack of adequate infrastructures, resources and management staff in the university education departments. According to the draft plan, intending secondary school teachers must obtain credits in "education" and in teaching methods besides qualifying for the traditional licentiat in their disciplines. It is assumed that the restructuring of universities into departments will facilitate this development.

There is a prevailing theory in Spain as in many OECD countries that the teaching profession is indivisible, and that similar training methods should be used for all teachers, whose basic store of knowledge needs to be the same. The problem is to know to what extent consideration should be given to the special characteristics of each level. Current practice reflects the approach that there is no real need to take account of such characteristics, and the principle applied is rather "whoever can do more can do less"; it is true that university graduates in Spain are recruited as teachers at EGB level.

The idea is gaining ground that the whole system of teacher training should be standardized and integrated within the university, which would be consistent with the EGB teacher training colleges having been attached to universities. Naturally, this will cause some problems. Will the present centres be integrated into the first university cycle? This would give teachers a first university cycle of three years' general basic training followed by training in pedagogy.

What form should this pedagogical training take, since it seems that it would have to be both general and specific at the same time? Would it be geared to the practicalities of teaching only, or would it also be theoretical and so enable teachers to follow, if not participate, in the evolution of educational ideas? How long would it last? How should the division be made between specialised subject-matter training and pedagogical training? How could relations between the faculties responsible for educational theory and practice and the education departments be put on a better footing? Is the department not going to be cut off completely from the practical side? How can it be enabled to pursue research activities which could help both the authorities and teachers to solve their organisational and pedagogical problems?

The Spanish authorities, universities and teachers are confronted with a series of choices common to most countries that are not easy to make: how to co-ordinate academic and pedagogical training; how much importance to give each; whether this should depend on the age of the pupils, and if so, in accordance with which age brackets? For the term "level" is ambiguous. Is it considered that in EGB there should be just one single pedagogical approach throughout, given that the 6-to-11 year-olds have one teacher only, and the 11-to-14 year-olds have different specialised teachers? Will compulsory schooling for 14-to-16 year-olds not require a more discriminating educational approach? In addition, what sort of preparation is to be given to teachers who will be working in a system of education endeavouring to be open and to encourage participation, the ability to listen, discuss, administer, work in a team and so on? Will a standardized training system mean that all teachers are trained to the same academic or pedagogical level and both from pre-school to the end of upper secondary education? If different levels are envisaged, where should the dividing lines be? at 6, 12, 14 or 16 years?

How is training in psychology, pedagogy and educational theory and practice and special methods to be co-ordinated? Should there be a standard basic training comprising, for example:

-   a uniform level of instruction in general pedagogy, child and adolescent psychology and development, introduction to the theoretical problems of educational research and its methods, introduction to applied research;
-   the same basic instruction concerning social and cultural problems;
-   an equivalent level of instruction in general methodology and specialisation in special methods appropriate to different levels and subjects.

Should a standardized career system be envisaged, giving teachers occupational mobility after the appropriate extra training either in basic pedagogy or in the specialisation chosen?

In short, the current norms seem too general, given that they have to cover a wide and varied field and pupils from age 3 to 18-19, from infancy to adulthood, and do not seem to take sufficient account of developments in educational theory whether as regards its role as a fundamental discipline or as a technological and rational instrument for influencing educational practice.

In-service training

Great efforts have been made in this field, including: creation of a programme for the in-service training of EGB teachers organised by the Distance University; creation of Departments of Educational Studies in each university with the dual task of undertaking educational research and organising working groups and INSET courses; creation in 1983 of a network of "Centres for the Study and Exchange of Ideas about Pedagogical Reforms" (CEIRES) for the primary school level which, in 1984, were integrated in the network of Teachers Centres. The latter are decentralised or locally run. They are financed by the Ministry of Education and Science with additional support from the authorities in the Autonomous Regions as well as the local authorities. Their purpose is to serve the needs of the teachers in their catchment areas by helping them adapt the curriculum to local conditions and to organise working groups of teachers, INSET courses, documentation, audiovisual and other services as required. Teachers' associations also organise INSET courses.

We were informed that the present activities of the ICEs in retraining non-university teachers may be transferred to the CEPs. We feel that such a decision would be unfortunate since it would deprive the ICEs of sustained contact with what is actually going on in the classroom, and with teachers actively involved in their work. A system under which the ICEs were closely associated with CEP activities would seem to us an effective way of bringing ICEs out of their isolation and of overcoming the tendency of which we often heard them accused, namely, that of taking refuge in theory to the detriment of practice. In our view, an imaginative programme of applied educational research involving constant collaboration between ICEs and teachers would constitute a strongly supportive instrument for the educational development model that the government is endeavouring to introduce and which we have analysed above.

Resources

Decentralisation and the delegation of certain responsibilities in the field of education from the centre to the Autonomous Regions and from the Regions to the local authorities seem to us to constitute an opportunity to develop a widely implemented and flexible system of in-service training. The fact must be faced, however, that such a development, which seems to us absolutely indispensable in Spain, will require significant investment in both manpower and materials. Action of this type does more harm than good if it only goes half-way. We feel therefore that bolder but meticulous planning is essential in the entire field of initial and in-service teacher training.

VIII

HIGHER EDUCATION

Rapid growth

With a student population of over 700 000 and more than 40 000 teachers, thirty universities (including three Catholic and one private), four polytechnic universities and a large number of university schools and higher technical schools, Spain ranks among the leading countries in the world with extensive higher education systems. The number of students has practically doubled during the last fifteen years. A few new universities were created over the same period, as were a series of new faculties and schools, in order to correct the uneven regional distribution of opportunities – 47 per cent of university places are still concentrated in Madrid and Barcelona – and meet the increasingly pressing individual and social demand. Expansion has also been a means of injecting new blood into very traditional universities. Among the new institutions are an "open" university and polytechnics.

The expansion of higher education, as in other OECD countries, is a direct consequence of the top-to-bottom democratisation of the education system. As we have already pointed out, following the first radical changes in the education system in 1970, all sectors expanded rapidly, especially secondary education. The stress at this level, which persists to this day, was placed precisely on preparing young people for university (Secondary Leaving Certificate + University Foundation Course: BUP + COU). In addition, the "competition for credentials" and the modernisation of the economy and administration created the conditions for unprecedented growth. The authorities did not, and still do not, see grounds for disquiet. They do not propose to halt or at least channel the growth in given directions, except for places in medical schools and to some extent in higher technical colleges. They are unwilling to intervene in the belief, rightly, that no system of selection is fair, whether it be administrative or through imposition of a *numerus clausus*. Selection does take place, however, on completion of the first year of university study. Moreover, the 1983 university reform bill provides for the possibility of introducing special entrance examinations for courses other than medicine. For the time being, however, the present entrance examinations pose no problems for students who have completed the BUP and COU, the pass rate being over 90 per cent.

Candidates require no more than an average mark of 5 out of 10 in the final COU examinations and that includes marks obtained in BUP, which are subjective and biased in his or her favour. A *numerus clausus* has now been imposed on entrance to medicine and examinations for the schools of nursing and EGB teacher training are considered to be more or less selective. A draft clause on university entrance was included in the new Law of

50

University Reform (LRU – *Ley de Reforma Universitaria* – 1983), but as yet it remains non-operational, no doubt because it concerns a socially and politically delicate issue.

The expansion of the higher education system and the large number of enrolments are not viewed *per se* as a major economic burden, especially as the government is making strenuous and largely successful efforts to allocate increased resources. Indeed, with an overall student/teacher ratio of 16.14 in higher education generally and 21.5 in the universities, Spain has already reached the level of most advanced industrialised countries. In addition, roughly 100 million dollars have been invested in the year 1984-85 alone in order to ensure that teaching standards shall be more or less equal throughout the country. The government is committed to this policy of equalisation by the new University Reform Act of 1983, the main provisions of which will take effect as from 1985-86.

A distorted demand

Although many disciplines are covered, student demand for higher education is distorted. On the one hand, it is biased towards long-cycle studies of a more or less theoretical character and, on the other hand, it is focused on disciplines such as Law, Philosophy, Humanities, Medicine and Biology. The number of enrolments in the higher technical colleges has been falling and yet they turn out the type of graduate that the economy needs. The prevailing demand is governed by the "prestige" of academic titles and the economic advantages accruing to certain professions, notably medicine, rather than to realistic career opportunities and the essential needs of the country. Clearly, much more effective information and counselling procedures are called for.

No one appears to wish to defend the present position which is deemed unfair, skewed and of questionable value even in economic terms. The question is whether a sweeping reform should precede or follow critical reconsideration of the structure and organisation of university studies with a view to ending the present bias towards more "traditional" courses and promoting a constructive balance among the many types and branches of studies, simultaneously taking into account the geographical distribution of institutions and their available facilities. As we have already argued, in Chapter V, university reform cannot be dissociated from the reform of the structure, organisation and content of the second cycle of secondary education for the 16 to 19 age group, which will have to be conceived with a common purpose in mind while still pursuing its specific objectives.

The most important break-through has already occurred with the inclusion of short-cycle post-secondary education within the universities. Even if, as we have pointed out in the chapter on teacher training, full integration has not been achieved and the faculties and university schools remain isolated from each other, the principle seems to have been accepted and can be taken further by giving equal weight, even in terms of duration, to more professional or more academic kinds of subjects and establishing a system of credits or circuits to ensure equality of access.

A high drop-out rate and long courses

The phenomenal rise in university enrolments since about 1970 reflects the country's egalitarian desire to repudiate the elitism of the past and offer places to all who qualify; but that equitable outcome has been bought at a price. The price is a very severe drop-out rate, especially during the first year (70 per cent in the Madrid Polytechnic) and a low completion rate. The mass intake of the first year adversely affects the quality of the courses on offer.

High drop-out rates are a feature of all countries where there is not a *numerus clausus* on university admissions. Spain, however, has a second problem. It is that, on the average, students take longer to complete a degree than their counterparts in the rest of Europe. This is due to two causes. First, the degree courses are long to begin with: almost all courses last five to six years. The arguments put forward to explain the long duration are based on traditionalist and corporatist considerations. The real reason lies in the way higher education is organised. Secondly, students are allowed to repeat courses that they fail and to try four times to pass the examination at the end of each course. The perennial student has thus become a familiar figure. About 40 per cent of students overall repeat courses, the percentage of repeats rising to as high as 70 per cent in Science disciplines.

Reform projects and problems

Contrary to its impact on other educational levels, the General Law of Education of 1970 did not stipulate any major reform of university-level education, whether as regards structures or processes, but it did contain some important provisions. The major innovation was the inclusion within universities of short-cycle courses that did not previously have university status, such as those for technical engineers and for teachers of the first two levels of Basic Education (as described in the foregoing chapter). Thus, higher education was divided into three levels leading to the titles of *diplomado*, "technical architect", or "technical engineer" (short cycle), *licenciado* (second cycle) and *doctor* (third cycle). At the same time, two types of establishments were defined: university schools (*Escuelas Universitarias*) for short-cycle degrees, and faculties and higher schools for the traditional university degrees (three cycles). The title of *diplomado* was also to be granted to students completing the first cycle of the traditional courses, though this had no professional career value.

The law considered "Departments" to be the basic unit for organising teaching and research under discrete disciplines, but no action was taken until recently when the departmental principle was adopted in the recent LRU which is now being implemented. Meanwhile, between 1970 and 1983 several new subjects were incorporated in the universities within specialised faculties: Fine Arts, Information Technology, Data Processing, Sociology, Psychology, or in University Schools: Librarianship and Documentation, Physiotherapy, Social Work. Several faculties were also sub-divided into more specialised disciplines.

From the point of view of rational planning, there is still too much duplication of curricula, piecemeal organisation of disciplines and fragmentation of different subjects into several years' study. Each faculty within the same university develops its own fundamental disciplines – an irrational procedure that will not ensure the attainment of acceptable standards. It is true that the situation differs in the polytechnics and newly created universities, although we noted a tendency that needs to be watched for them to start aping the traditional universities.

The system of higher education, which corresponds more or less with the university system, is now undergoing a profound and in some respects controversial reform. The LRU was approved in Parliament with little dissent and will be enforced gradually. To the effects of that law must be added the effects of other laws concerning the reorganisation of the public services which have important repercussions on teaching careers (incompatibilities, retirement, etc.) as well as a recent government decree that elaborates certain clauses of the LRU, reorganises the third university cycle and regulates the granting of the PhD degree.

Although the contents and thrust of these legal instruments are consonant with contemporary university models, functions and objectives, their acceptance is far from universal.

Newspaper articles echo deep dissatisfaction among some academics about an alleged lack of prior consultation and the inclusion of certain measures that are considered too difficult to apply or even "demagogic". Specific criticisms are made of the so-called departmentalisation of the traditional "faculties" and the reduction of the university teaching career to two almost equivalent levels with titles – *catedratico* and *titular* – significantly different from the world-wide designations of "full" and "associate" professors, in keeping with the "title fever" common in other Latin countries.

Several thousand holders of doctorates, many of whom are quite young, rose to the position of *titulares* by passing a simple "maturity test" (*prueba de idoneidad*). The resulting levelling of titles, salaries and responsibilities, which conferred tenure on the vast majority of staff formerly on renewable contracts, evoked angry outcries from the oldest *catedraticos* who, without contesting the right to tenure, felt that too hasty promotions would affect the quality of the universities and their future standing and deplored the fact that experience, specialisation and scholarly achievement were no longer to be given appropriate distinctive rewards. Naturally, counter reactions were also expressed by many candidates for vacancies as *titulares* who did not succeed in the public competitions for posts, although it had been officially announced that a sufficient number of vacancies would soon be created which would be open to public competition.

It is not surprising to find this type of reaction in universities that are, after all, mirrors of society at large, but it is hard for external observers to judge and comment on the soundness of arguments that are usually couched in general terms. Some reactions are either conservative or even ideological in nature whereas others reflect group interests or personal ambitions for power or benefits. Common sense can scarcely prevail amid such special pleadings.

Curiously enough, critics from both camps complain about arbitrary decision-making. Now, participation in the preparation of laws that affect a community or society is, naturally, a desirable concomitant of policy-making in a democracy. But participation cannot easily be made constructive in a representative system that coexists with strong corporate tendencies and vested rights and interests. Thus, it is highly probable that if it had been subjected to a process of widespread internal discussion in the universities, the LRU would never have been promulgated, or so watered down as to be ineffectual.

What is certain is that opposition and constraints are powerful so that enactment of the law is no guarantee of its full enforcement. For example, the establishment of departments may prove difficult in several old universities which have been structured traditionally as faculties, and it may be argued whether it is worth coercing them to adopt what is viewed as an unnatural reform. Furthermore, the development of research, which is the *raison d'être* of a departmental structure, requires facilities – offices, research laboratories, etc. – which do not exist in some faculties and which the change to a departmentalised structure by itself cannot provide.

These are constraints that will require considerable effort to overcome. In the end, the only solution may be to replace "old" by "new" universities, not only in terms of staff and spirit but of physical facilities as well – new buildings, equipment and support, without which the reform can be scarcely more than a paper tiger.

The problems of teaching and research are even more delicate. Security of tenure has to be assured without diminishing quality and this gives rise to a double risk for the future: first, the youthfulness of the staff is bound to lead to some inertia as a critical mass of staff stay in post until their distant date of retirement; secondly, security of tenure is no guarantee of quality and the trend to fill vacancies for *titulares* may lead to mediocrity and to conditions that will discourage the most able academics, thereby making it more difficult simultaneously to foster excellence and to respect the autonomy of the institutions with its foreseen democratic forms of government limited to the participation of a few.

In other words, the new measures require to be reinforced by the provision of new facilities, equipment, supporting staff and incentives to undertake research and care for quality. University staff will be encouraged to perform well where there is the possibility of study abroad, cooperation with other countries and more frequent meetings among academic peers. The need to stimulate creative research may also require the deliberate opening up of Spanish universities to distinguished foreign professors and researchers, especially in view of Spain's accession to the EEC. In fact, the regulations do permit the appointment of visiting lecturers or professors who may be made permanent members of staff.

There are still striking differences among the various universities in terms of resources and academic quality, differences mainly stemming from historical causes and the resource problems inevitably facing new institutions. Corrective measures are required, therefore, in order to establish a good competitive spirit based on the pursuit of quality and freedom from geographical, political or other constraints.

It would be Utopian to advocate exactly equal conditions in diverse environments and institutions, but some anomalies do require attention. One is the wide range of the percentage of total university costs covered by students' fees. This may simply reflect the fact that some universities are crowded, but it also shows that no extra money is forthcoming from the State to match high enrolments. Although the available information may well be inaccurate or partial, it seems to us that it might be wise to introduce a new resource allocation model, which could take into account the different situations and gradually iron out the more glaring disparities.

It is inevitable, of course, and even desirable, that some institutions should receive preferential treatment, particularly if they succeed in developing centres of excellence in specific academic areas. It is also evident that technological institutions will always be more expensive to run than those which concentrate on the humanities and the social sciences, but this particular disparity could be catered for in the new resource allocation model.

The research function

The Background Report of the Spanish authorities contains no information on the research component of the universities' activities, although this has now become extremely important because of changes in the teaching career pattern and the avowed necessity for the nation of facing the challenge of technological change. It is acknowledged by the authorities that scientific research in Spain has not so far received sufficient attention and financial support, that present isolated research efforts are not adequately coordinated and evaluated and that the contribution of research to social and economic progress has been negligible.

The national development envisaged over the next few years will necessarily have science as one of its main propellants if Spain wishes to increase its competitive capacity in international markets. This will entail major changes in the organisation and functioning of the universities. Leaving aside sterile arguments about the respective values of pure and applied research, one conclusion is undeniable: it is the universities that must be responsible for the initial training of top level scientific manpower, and whatever objectives are set by national plans for scientific research and technological development, the promotion of advanced research at the universities is a definite priority. But for this purpose large investments will have to be made simply because the traditional Spanish university has not been designed to support any activities other than classical teaching. Offices, libraries, laboratories, stores, as well as technical and administrative staff, will have to be provided and a steady level of activity will have to be achieved before the universities across the nation can be expected to play a more decisive research and development role. It would be wrong to push for activities alien to their vocation and unfair to ask for more than they can offer within the present constraints.

In Spain research and development activities strongly favour industrial research, as is shown by the correlation of the percentage of total expenditure relative to GDP and the percentage of expenditure in industrial research and development relative to total expenditure as compared to most OECD countries (see Figure 1). Although the data available refer to the period 1975-1980 (1976 in the case of Spain) and a substantial effort has been undertaken over the last few years, it is unlikely that the distortion has been completely corrected. The figure clearly shows that highly advanced countries seek to deploy and harmonize the development of industrial and non-industrial research. In order to follow that trend Spain

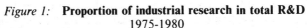

Figure 1: **Proportion of industrial research in total R&D**
1975-1980

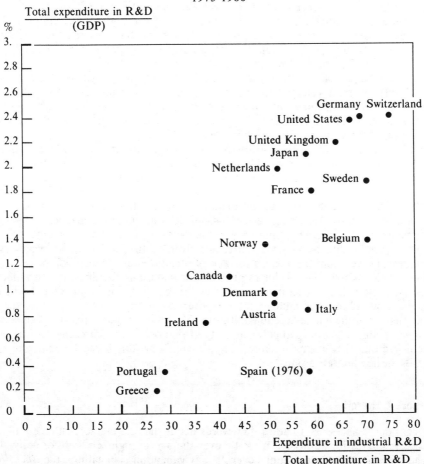

Source: V.B. Goncalves and J.M.G. Caraça, in *Anàlise Social,* vol. xx, pp. 115-124, Lisbon, 1984.

must not only increase the percentage of GDP dedicated to research and development but invest in the promotion of its general scientific capacity, i.e. in the development of the scientific potential of the universities and other research institutions.

It must be stressed that the government is, indeed, making some effort to encourage the universities to engage in research. So far, however, only 5 per cent of the total higher education budget is earmarked for this purpose, specifically for applied research, thereby signalling a distinction between types of research that is at least questionable given the overall objectives and functions of these institutions.

Another problem, that deserves some comment, is the rigid separation between services, industry, the universities and autonomous scientific institutes. There is, in consequence, little interplay between university research on the one hand and the actual requirements of the economy and society on the other. Certain legal and other barriers are inhibiting factors. Qualified specialists must opt for a mainstream career either in a university or in business or in the civil service, and the possibilities for cooperation in different activities are limited or not financially attractive. Hence most of the discussion about the need for university reform takes for granted the traditional order, that is, universities and higher education institutions that are largely separate from scientific research institutions, business and the civil service. Furthermore, staff in autonomous scientific institutions do not enjoy the same teaching status as university teachers, so there is low job mobility.

Given the strength of the old university tradition, radical change will be hard to accomplish. Nevertheless, a younger generation of specialists is being developed slowly and most higher education teaching staff now have doctorates. The teaching staff "pyramid" remains too "narrow" at the top, there being some 2 000 full professors, a relatively small number in comparison with the total teaching force of 40 000.

The efforts of the government and the Ministry of Education and Science, particularly by means of the new LRU, have undoubtedly shaken up the situation in higher education and that is very desirable even if there is cause for concern for the older and more traditionally organised universities. At first sight this might seem paradoxical since the new Act also increases the universities' autonomy, giving them more rights than ever before. On the other hand, the new law will transform a great deal in Spanish universities, in particular as regards the participation of the external community in their management and development. To this end "Social Councils" are being set up in each university that will have wide powers and include representatives from the various sections of society. Each Council will be responsible for financial planning and control, for establishing or abolishing faculties and for allocating vacancies. At present it is difficult to gauge how far-reaching this improvement will be in practice, but it should result in much greater exposure to society and the economy, and vice-versa, and this is, in principle, a laudable initiative. The great danger is that the Councils will become too parochial according to political party affiliations. To avoid such perverse effects it is to be hoped that their composition will be sufficiently broadly-based to include representatives of all the key interest groups.

The Distance University

We consider it necessary to add a few words about the role of the Distance University (UNED). Candidates for admission must be over the age of eighteen and normally should possess the *Bachillerato*. Mature adults over 25 may gain admission without the *Bachillerato* and many do so. In addition, there is a "gateway" programme designed to help candidates attain an adequate entrance level. In 1984-85 there were 49 000 regular students and 93 000 students in all.

The Distance University functions unequivocally like a residential university in terms of both the academic rigour of its courses and its system of evaluation: this is shown by the high failure rate of 70 per cent in the first year and 20 per cent in the second and third year and the fact that the normal period required for obtaining a degree is seven to eight years. We were also told that its graduates obtain very good results in the civil service entrance examinations.

It may then be asked what are the distinctive features of the Distance University. We could distinguish several. First, its admission requirements are flexible enough to permit mature entrance; a special entrance examination for adults over 25 years old can be taken for all Spanish universities but applies particularly in practice to UNED. Secondly, it enables adults who live in remote areas or who work irregular hours to study towards a degree. Thirdly, it has a broadly-based and flexible curriculum. Fourthly, it uses a wide variety of methods. Fifthly, courses are organised into a series of modules. Sixthly, it operates fifty study centres, including five outside Spain, that, incidentally, serve as cultural centres in the communities where they are located. Finally, it is claimed to be more economic than the residential universities, despite severe wastage in the first three years. The students pay fees and the operations are largely self-financing.

Like the Open University in the United Kingdom this university designs its course material and instructional methods with technical competence. Its textbooks are well planned; it provides video-cassettes; it uses broadcasting by radio at the peak hours of 8-10.30 p.m., but does not use television; it employs tutors to work closely with each student; it applies a system of continual assessment.

We are in no position to comment on the absolute quality of the courses and students but the Distance University does appear to be performing a valuable service. Adults who opted out of the education system are able to resume their studies, many finding that it offers the only way of upgrading their qualifications. Thus, its students comprise a large number of civil servants, including many teachers, and five hundred prison inmates. One might question why no fewer than 18 000 students are reading law. Is this used by many as a general-purpose rather than a professional course? We also noted that it is catering largely for adults below middle age; the average age is thirty and falling. Is there a possibility that its students will become mostly young adults who prefer to have a job and study simultaneously rather than to attend a university on a full-time basis?

Some recommendations

Despite the major problems to be tackled Spanish higher education is being buffeted by an exhilarating wind of change. The examiners offer the following suggestions for consideration as a contribution to the debate on future orientations and in the context of the ever-increasing challenges posed by the irresistible development of science and technology on a world-wide scale. The order in which they are presented does not reflect priorities:

  i) Courses should be shortened so that their duration does not exceed four or five years; the necessity for two cycles should also be reviewed, that is, the need for a two-tier system. The latter, however, is obviously largely dependent on the repercussion of changes planned at secondary school level.

 ii) There should be a closer articulation between secondary and higher education curricula so that university teaching time is not taken up with repeating the courses and correcting the defects of secondary education, although wide gaps of content and level must also be avoided. Secondary education should provide a broad general and work-referenced education to all children.

iii) The career profiles provided by university education should be broadened so as to match scientific and technical developments taking place in the external world. Narrow specialisation should be removed from the standard curriculum and taught at Master's and Doctorate levels (third cycle).

iv) Courses should be more closely adapted to the needs of the economy and public service and students better equipped for their future occupations. This implies the creation of an efficient system of higher education planning and an end to uncontrolled and autonomous development. The present concentration of students in the humanities and medical faculties might then be gradually reduced.

v) Likewise, the development of higher education should be dovetailed into the future industrial reorganisation and modernisation of the country.

vi) The regional development of higher education is also a vital factor in stimulating growth in the more backward regions of the country. This implies the possible relocation of some university centres, adapting each region's higher education provision to its own perceived needs, even if this does not mean exclusive specialisation.

vii) While the overall number of students does not seem excessive, tighter selection should be introduced at the admission stage. This would reduce the number of students who spend too many years in obtaining their degrees and also lower the drop-out rate. As many enrolled students as possible should complete their courses, not only so as to reduce the cost of unproductive learning but also to enlarge the national stock of advanced qualifications.

viii) In the interests of better quality teaching and ensuring that teachers remain constantly aware of the problems and changes taking place in the economy and society, professional mobility should be encouraged within the civil service, industry, commerce and university nexus and cooperation should be stimulated on a more flexible basis than at present. The teaching load of staff should be reorganised so as to permit commitments to independent scientific institutions or to industry.

ix) The activities of scientific institutions and universities should be integrated so that universities have both a scientific and teaching role and are not just teaching establishments. In practice, this implies that no new faculty should be set up or existing faculty supported which does not engage in scientific inquiry and research with adequate resources. In this way, the quality of university teaching could be raised and a "critical mass" of researchers could be formed capable of tackling the increasingly complex problems arising from the impact of new technology on Spain and the consequences of its entry into the European Economic Community.

Part Two

RECORD OF THE REVIEW MEETING

Paris, 5th December 1985

The Chairman, Mr. Brenner, declared that the OECD examination of the education system of Spain was very timely. The frankness with which the CIDE had approached important issues in the preparation of the national Background Report, at a moment when Spanish society was opening up to a wave of change, was indicative of great confidence in the future.

Mr. Milutinović, on behalf of the examiners, stated that the process of reform of the education system in Spain was not only broad and deep but also very rapid, so that important developments had taken place even since the examiners' visit only ten months earlier. He hoped that the Spanish delegation would be able to brief the Committee on these developments.

Mr. Maravall, Minister of Education and Science, emphasized the vital role of education in the programme for modernisation of Spanish society, underway since 1982. The Education Act of 1970 and the Laws of 1978 had been important milestones but provision remained insufficient in many areas: compulsory schooling was inadequately endowed in quantitative terms; there were many gaps in vocational education and the universities had scarcely been touched by reform. The present administration had four more or less equal priorities. *First, efforts were being made to develop a coherent legislative framework*; two laws had been passed, one governing the university sector, the other, the non-university sector. Parliament was debating a third major piece of legislation to cover scientific and technological research.

With regard to higher education, the intention had been to make the universities, traditionally managed by a centralised bureaucracy, more diverse and more competitive. Now, each had become autonomous with its own statutes. In order that they be responsive to the needs of society, two instruments had been created: a national council on which all universities had seats and a social council on which community and economic interest groups were represented. The government had also sought to strengthen the research function of the universities by replacing the traditional faculties with a departmental system, developing the post-graduate sector, introducing new procedures for recruiting staff, financing and encouraging research, renewing outdated curricula and degrees, substantially increasing financial resources and, finally, democratising access to higher education through an ambitious policy for students' grants.

The law relating to the education system outside the universities was approved following an intense public debate. It set forth a general plan, formulating basic rights, establishing participatory roles in educational institutions for parents, pupils and teachers and regulating the private sector, which catered for a third of enrolments. Its main objectives were: free compulsory education for all through an integrated co-educational structure covering public and private institutions; equality of access with priority given according to family income and place of residence; better use of public funds through general programming of teaching and rationalisation of staffing through the help of school councils, on which sat parents, teachers, pupils and administrators; raising quality by improving building stock, pupil/teacher ratios and teaching qualifications and by involving parents and teachers in decision-making, in relation, for example, to the appointment of staff and budgetary matters; protecting certain constitutional liberties such as freedom of conscience, parental choice of schools, non-discrimination and so forth.

A second major priority was to extend and enhance the state education system. 1 600 000 new places had been created over the last three years. One out of six pupils was attending a newly created or refurbished school. Provision for four and five year-olds had also been developed considerably, with 80 per cent coverage for four year-olds and 97 per cent for five year-olds.

The third area of priority was support for the disadvantaged. There were three major programmes. One was a compensatory programme, linking 84 000 small schools by means of a network of 404 resource centres designing courses to assist fourteen and fifteen year-old school-leavers unable to find a job, and organising literacy classes for members of the gipsy community. Another scheme had increased the resources available for grants so as to equalise opportunity and to compensate those who chose to continue their studies rather than go immediately to work. Then there was a programme for helping the physically and mentally handicapped, seven out of ten of whom were to be enabled to attend school.

The fourth and by no means the least of the government's priorities was to improve the very quality of the education system. It was essential to reduce the failure rate. In many respects this was a socio-economic problem, of which the government had taken account in determining its policies. However, since the content of the curriculum also had to be adjusted to the needs of individuals, the whole of basic general education up to 14 years was under review. Given the intention to extend compulsory attendance beyond that age, the curriculum for older pupils would also be made more relevant to the reality of life outside school. It was also essential to improve teaching through better provision of in-service training. Staff salaries had been increased by 41 per cent over the last two years. Modifications were about to be introduced which would provide for the training of teachers in such areas as pre-schooling, dealing with handicapped children, music, languages and use of computers. A new network of training institutions, accessible geographically to all teachers, was being installed. Since the examiners' visit a special committee of experts had been convened to study how best to establish a professional career structure. The significance of statistical indicators was never easy to assess but it was still noteworthy that since the government had begun to implement its policies the number of pupils obtaining a leaving certificate had increased from 66 to 72 per cent.

Education was a vital factor in the country's future. Educational reforms must be designed to improve the quality of life of each young person so as to assure him or her a better future. The Spanish government, despite the many obstacles it faced, had set this as a prime objective for the long term.

I

POLICY-MAKING, FINANCING, PLANNING AND IMPLEMENTATION

Question 1

The comprehensive Background Report prepared by the Spanish authorities describes a formidable number of reforms, in all sectors of the education system, that are already under way or anticipated. The Minister himself has spoken of the feasibility of this all-embracing reform process "maturing" within five to seven years. The question arises whether all the reforms can be implemented in such a short space of time; for example, is it really feasible to expand the pre-school sector so as to match all the potential demand for places? The examiners would be interested to know whether the Ministry is assuming that, in practice, there must be a hierarchy of priorities. If so, what are the three or four most urgent priorities?

Question 2

Whatever those priorities, the various reforms necessitate increased capital expenditure on buildings and equipment and a greater investment in the training and retraining of teachers. Moreover, the reforms will lead immediately to increased enrolments among the 14-16 age group and a knock-on effect among the 16-19 age group. How will the necessary financial resources be mobilised to sustain such a large quantitative expansion?

Question 3

The Ministry of Education is shedding much of its power and many of its administrative functions to the Autonomous Regions while also carrying out internal reforms of its structure and procedures. Nevertheless, there still seems to be an absence of indicative overall planning and of instruments for evaluating the effects of major reforms. Are there any proposals to make good this deficiency? Is there a case, for example, for broadening the role of the CIDE by adding an explicit planning and evaluation function to its existing research and information functions?

Question 4

Against the background of the evolving and complex process of decentralising educational responsibilities to the Autonomous Regions it is the declared national policy to maintain equality of access and resources throughout the country. How is it intended to implement this policy in view of the desire of the Autonomous Regions to establish and pursue their own educational priorities and in view of the wide range of their financial capacities? Will differences in rates of population growth, educational achievement, and adult literacy be taken into account? What administrative and financial instruments are in place to ensure an equitable nation-wide balance among the different regional priorities? Specifically, will students be enabled to go to the universities of their choice and will teachers, in practice as well as in principle, be able to move from one province to another?

Question 5

Vocational training is the concern not only of the Ministry of Education but also of the Ministry of Labour and several other ministries. Research and development, cultural programmes and compensatory learning opportunities are also the concern of other ministries. What machinery exists or is envisaged for ensuring inter-ministerial coordination of related policies and programmes? Specifically, how are educational and employment policies to be harmonized in the future?

Question 6

The Spanish authorities are strongly in favour of the close involvement of parents and the wider community in the running and daily existence of the schools but, in practice, at the school level everything appears to depend upon good will and voluntary efforts, even though parental involvement is regulated by the law. What measures have been taken or are envisaged for stimulating parental and community participation to an effective level?

Question 7

Private schools are responsible for a substantial part of educational provision and it continues to be public policy to subsidise their capital and recurrent expenditures to a very large extent on condition that they fulfil prescribed conditions. How do the authorities view the future of the private schools and their relationship with the public school system? In particular, do they foresee any modifications in the present system of financing private schools such as fiscal exemptions and low interest rate loans for the purpose of construction and purchase of equipment?

Mr. Frausto da Silva submitted the examiners' first set of questions with a few brief comments. He stressed the need for educational planning and for the collection of reliable quantitative data. Admittedly, the technocratic approach to educational planning had been widely discredited since the 1960s but there must still be a planning strategy and a hierarchy of priorities. Thus, Spain would do well to integrate the various reforms being implemented in each cycle of the system and remedy an apparent absence of coordination between ministries. Next, he wondered how the government was going to reconcile its objectives of decentralisation and equality of access to education. It would be necessary, by one means or another, to manage the system overall, while at the same time granting genuine autonomy to regions of varying size and influence. Lastly, he noted that parents were not taking up the opportunity to participate in school management. Had the authorities conceived any new measures of encouragement since the examiners' visit?

The Minister agreed that coordination and planning were absolutely essential. Resources were necessarily limited but the budget had been increased from 532 million pesetas in 1982 to approximately 965 million in 1986, that is, from 2.6 to 3.2 per cent of GDP. Still greater support would be given in the future. Given this level of funding, it had been possible to establish the priorities referred to earlier, above all the extension and improvement of basic education and restructuring of higher education.

Other priorities included enlarging the provision before and after compulsory schooling. The authorities wished to develop pre-school education for the entire three-to-six age group and initiatives were being launched to improve the curriculum in the *escuelas infantiles*. Another pressing requirement was the reform of the lower secondary sector up to sixteen, and the upper secondary sector up to eighteen. It was intended to prolong compulsory schooling up to the age of sixteen. Naturally, this would entail major new expenditure but with the advent of an era of falling rolls it should be possible to ensure adequate standards of performance.

In order to cater for the entire fourteen-to-fifteen age group it would be necessary to create a further 250 000 places. This meant that considerable new resources would be required for public and private schooling and these two sectors would have to be better coordinated. Resources could be reallocated from compulsory education, where there was currently a surplus of 1 100 000 places. It would equally be possible to shift funding from another area that has not a high priority – namely, private vocational training for people over seventeen – which until now had been heavily subsidised.

Other problems were not related to resources so much as to planning, coordination and the competence of personnel. The process of decentralisation had led to 40 per cent of administrators and 55 per cent of teaching staff being transferred from the Ministry to six of the Autonomous Regions. Coordination would be maintained through a special council, chaired by the Minister himself, and also a State School Council on which the various sectors of education would be represented. The government would continue to have an important mandate regarding curricular development and control, maintenance of minimum standards and award of certificates. Similarly, the Universities Council, with representatives from the Autonomous Regions and presided over by the Minister, would have a major planning role.

The State would also continue to be responsible for ensuring equality of access and opportunity. Two main instruments existed for this purpose: the Inter-regional Compensatory Fund and a compensatory programme for education. Equal access to the universities was now governed by law. Teachers and civil servants were also free to move from one region to another and could apply for any post in the country.

Responsibility for vocational education and training was shared by the Ministries of Labour and Education. A new inter-ministerial commission had been set up since the examiners' visit. It was chaired by the two Ministers concerned and representatives of the trade unions and the employers were represented on it. Coordination had made it possible to agree on a coherent plan for vocational education. The long-term objective of stable employment for each young person required close cooperation between the two Ministries but educational goals would not be made subservient to the exigencies of the labour market.

Finally, to answer the question about parental involvement in the management of education, the law required that parents and staff be allowed to participate in the running of institutions in receipt of public funds. This included the appointment of teachers and heads (principals). A campaign had been launched, using the media, to inform the public about educational matters and to promote the idea of participation.

The delegate of the United Kingdom wanted to know how control of minimum standards would be exercised from the centre when evaluation was still to be left in the hands of individual teachers and schools. *The Swedish delegate* wondered whether the Autonomous Regions would have very wide scope for modifying educational programmes and, if so, whether this would not jeopardise the unifying function of compulsory schooling across the nation. Equally, might not decentralisation of university and training curricula impede the mobility of teachers?

Mr. Arango explained that mechanisms did exist to monitor standards. A national inspectorate undertook a yearly evaluation according to instructions from the Ministry. Efforts were made to standardize information flows between the schools and post-school institutions. Among other research institutions, there was the Centre for Educational Research and Documentation (CIDE), which carried out or commissioned periodic studies of different parts of the system. The Minister was considering introducing a standard test at the end of *Bachillerato* so as to be able to maintain rigorous standards of quality and evaluate pupils' performance. The State could also exercise control through its role as overseer of the selection and credentialling of teachers. Furthermore, it could impose basic curricular norms for teacher training on the universities so as to avoid any problems of mobility. Finally, it was worth emphasizing that the Ministry was empowered to establish throughout the country a common core for each subject in the curriculum.

The design of the main lines and elements of the system was the responsibility of the State, which decided the conditions that the curricula must satisfy and that were to apply to the award of nationally recognised certificates. This was in no way incompatible with the principle of diversity and freedom of choice implied by decentralisation. On the one hand, the Autonomous Regions had considerable latitude in curriculum development and the appointment of staff; on the other, national standards and requirements must be prescribed and fulfilled.

The Portuguese delegate was interested to know more about the role of the inspectorate which, according to the Background Report, was divided into three sections. It was the compensatory fund which intrigued *the Swiss representative*. Were resources distributed in single blocks for each region to decide how to use them, or were they attributed sector by sector on the basis of special needs? *The Canadian delegate*, pointing out that the degree to which government funding was earmarked conditioned its power to influence, was also greatly interested to know more about central contributions to regional budgets.

Mr. Arango replied that there were, indeed, three very different inspectorates. The General Inspection of Services was responsible for overseeing the normal working of all government departments. Then, the Technical Inspectorate for Education was mandated to monitor, supervise and, above all, evaluate the system. It had also developed a role as mediator or arbitrator between different parts of the system. As for the National Inspectorate, its role was to watch over the Autonomous Regions – their internal activities and their relations with the central authorities – in order to ensure compliance with legal and institutional requirements.

Regarding the question of compensatory funding, the process of decentralisation had not yet been fully implemented. The government was drafting a law to provide for the financing of the Autonomous Regions. Mechanisms would be introduced to offset the inequalities between regions. The function of the compensatory fund was to even out financial inequalities. Allocations were to be made on the basis of recognised disparities but the provinces were free to decide how to spend them, for example whether on education or public works. Of course, the State had also to ensure that enough resources were available to finance the requirements that it imposed from the centre. Since 1982, compensatory education programmes had also been designed, for instance, to help isolated rural schools, the unemployed, unqualified youngsters and the gipsy minorities. Grants and other mechanisms for equalising access to education were also controlled from the centre.

The German delegate remarked that central government influence on local educational policy was likely to wax and wane with changing economic fortunes and the availability of resources. His question concerned the sectoral conferences, mentioned in the examiners' report: what areas were they to cover and would they have a wide enough perspective to take into account problems extending beyond the scope of their particular sphere? *The French delegate* wished to know whether teachers were to be civil servants of the whole State or of one of the Autonomous Regions. In addition, would competitive examinations for the recruitment of teachers be organised in future at the national or the regional level?

In answer to the German representative's question about the sectoral conferences *Mr. Maravall* indicated that they were designed to provide a national forum for the discussion of problems relating to particular spheres. Each was presided over by the appropriate minister and the participants would represent the whole country. For example, there was a fiscal policy conference, chaired by the Minister of Finance, a health affairs one presided over by the Minister of Health and, of course, an educational conference under the presidency of the Minister of Education.

Mr. Arango answered the question by the French delegate about the status of teachers. Previous regulations were incoherent because they had been allowed to develop without being rationalised; there was, for example, no clearly defined career structure. Teachers had tended not to find this state of affairs very motivating. An Act, approved the previous year and covering the civil service in general, laid down certain general principles. The 25 categories of teachers were to be reduced to two, namely, primary and secondary level. A career structure was to be established and general criteria for this had been fixed. A group of experts would be reporting in January on plans for implementing this reform. In the meantime, teachers remained state civil servants with nation-wide rights, duties and also mobility. However, they were paid, supervised and administered by the Autonomous Regions. They were recruited through competitive examinations but these were also to be revised so that more credit might be given to genuine merit and experience rather than simply the ability to answer a set question on one particular day. Each region organised its own examinations but common norms and rules of selection had to be respected.

Mr. Lamo de Espinosa said that university teachers were also civil servants but with a special status. The number of categories of staff had been reduced from about 40 to no more than three. Access to posts was regulated by norms set by the State. The Autonomous Regions have no part in this as the universities themselves, having been granted full autonomy, were responsible, within the regulations, for their own budgetary, staff appointment and other policies.

The delegate of the Netherlands asked why, after years without controversy, there was now so much opposition to government policy from private school interest groups. When a country pursued a policy of decentralisation, private schools were likely to develop into superior, more prestigious institutions, closely linked with socially and economically privileged groups. He realised that many private schools in Spain were scarcely bastions of wealth, but had the Spanish delegation considered this threat to equality of opportunity?

Spain, according to *the Italian delegate*, had a particularly high proportion of private schools. Of course, this was only possible because of the 85 per cent financial support provided by the State. Did the authorities intend to maintain this system or was direct public management to be expanded? Did the private sector extend into higher education? Was it entirely confessional or were there other categories of independent institutions? In his country, said *the New Zealand delegate*, impoverished church schools were being subsidised and integrated into the national system. Did the situation in Spain reflect this experience? *The delegate of Luxembourg* wished to know whether the rationalisation of staff categories had included the private sector. Furthermore, what criteria had been used and how had the trade unions reacted? *The Australian delegate* wondered whether, as in his own country, it was possible to discern a higher demand for private education and training than for public provision.

The Minister explained that, historically, it was the private sector which had developed first, mainly under the aegis of the Church. Subsequently, public schooling had, of course, expanded to fill the roles assigned to it. The confessional institutions had found it necessary to employ secular staff because of the decline in religious vocations. Then, faced with a chronic shortage of funds, they had accepted subsidies from the State which, determined to fulfill its mandate of providing compulsory schooling for all, had been happy, in its turn, to take advantage of the possibilities offered by the private sector. Thus, an integrated system had been created, as in New Zealand.

The share of private education did indeed remain high but was actually less marked than in Belgium and Holland. As for higher education, the private sector was negligible. There were frictions between public and private schools, which went back long before 1982 and were due to many factors, not least the conditions imposed by the State in exchange for granting large subsidies. This had been a major obstacle in drafting the new constitution and it had only been overcome after a long process of consultation.

Two-thirds of private schooling was confessional. In general, it was of good quality and the government intended that, over the next three years, it should be one hundred per cent subsidised. No state money should be contributed to education that was not free and accessible to all. The Minister indicated that the enrolment share of public schooling had greatly increased over the last seven years, but he had no plans to restrict expenditure on the private sector. Changes would be introduced progressively and would arise largely from demographic trends.

With regard to the status of teachers, *Mr. Arango* said that the reform of the career structure and of the complicated system of categories had been well accepted since it was something that the professional unions had been demanding for many years. The private sector had not been affected, as it did not suffer from the same complexity. However, the government was bent on equalising salaries and working hours, seeing that private school teachers were at a slight disadvantage.

The Spanish delegation also indicated that the system of grants in force previously was quite unsatisfactory. In 1983, a royal decree established that grants should be concentrated on the post-compulsory level and compensate for loss of potential earnings. The State had made a considerable budgetary effort in that respect. University student grants had been considerably increased and measures had been taken to assist students from less privileged families.

II

EGB – THE BASIC SCHOOL

Question 8

There is widespread concern about the effectiveness of the basic or compulsory school, a concern that is dramatised by the high terminal failure rate of about 35 per cent of the age group. Various explanations for this failure rate were put forward to the examiners, including: the obsolescence of too much of the content; unimaginative teaching methods; lack of positive school leadership; some teachers' difficulty in coping with mixed-ability classes. What is the authorities' own diagnosis of the problems of the basic school and what remedies do they envisage for overcoming them?

Question 9

The rural school project, which impressed the examiners, should permit pupils at the primary and lower secondary level to obtain better academic results and to increase their stock of knowledge and skills. But where, locally, will they find occupational outlets on leaving school? Given the present lack of jobs in the rural areas they are more likely than not to migrate to the towns and increase the overpopulation there. Do the authorities see any possibility of tackling this problem by means of broadly-based local development schemes designed to generate employment and cultural activity?

Question 10

Age 11 to 16 cycle (three last years of EGB and two years of upper secondary education) have been chosen as the focus of major experimental programmes which will lead to changes in the preceding and succeeding cycles of schooling. The strategy chosen involves school-based experiments conducted by volunteer teachers who coordinate their activities regionally and nationally. Several problems arise: is the allotted time scale of three years sufficently long for the experiments to prove their worth? Has a precise and detailed plan been conceived for dissemination of essential findings and replication of good practice? Have the costs been fully estimated? Will sufficient resources be made available for consolidation and wide spread replication?

Question 11

The creation of a sub-directorate for Compensatory Education within the Directorate for Educational Advancement is designed to meet the special educational needs of young people and adults who, for a variety of reasons, including mental or physical handicaps, have not been able to acquire a sound basic education. What is distinctive about the approach of the sub-directorate and what are its priorities? What importance does it attach to the role of adult education centres and distance learning in serving the needs of disadvantaged groups? To what extent does it address the need for adult training and retraining courses against the prevailing background of high unemployment?

Mr. Vanbergen stated that basic general education (EGB) was clearly considered by the Spanish authorities to be of the highest priority. The examiners summed up the main objectives in this area under five headings: to give the whole population a common basic education; to increase the effectiveness of schools; to increase equality of opportunity by aiming for equality of outcomes; to promote economic and social development; to strengthen the democratic system.

However, the authorities had also to face five major problems. First, the expansion of provision had demanded a quantitative effort of a high order. Secondly, it had been essential to raise the quality of education; to that end, a development model based on experimentation and the participation of teachers, parents and the local authorities had been adopted. Thirdly, there was the question of structure; should the school-leaving age be extended to sixteen and, if so, how should the new system of primary and secondary education be segmented? In the fourth place, the Spanish government was coping with the problem of regional disparities through an active policy of decentralisation, including vigorous efforts to develop rural schools. Fifthly, teachers' qualifications had to be upgraded.

The Minister replied that there appeared to have been a steady rise in the quality of basic schooling even before the present administration had assumed power. The rate of young people not obtaining a school diploma had fallen from 35 to 27.5 per cent. It was, however, not easy to judge the reality behind the figures, given that individual teachers using different criteria and objectives were responsible for the assessment of pupils. The figure was high by international standards, but comparison with Belgium, the Netherlands, Italy, Switzerland and the United Kingdom had shown that Spanish pupils were not lagging behind at that age.

Two important factors affected the quality of the system. On the one hand, socio-economic factors had a clear influence; failure rates were higher among pupils from less privileged neighbourhoods and family backgrounds. On the other, the curricula were not adapted to real needs and teachers required better training for the posts they occupied. A series of measures had been introduced to overcome socio-economic obstacles through such means as extra support for rural schools and compensatory programmes for drop-outs of fourteen to fifteen. Efforts were also being made at the pre-school level to stimulate intellectual development from an early age. In addition, children with mild handicaps were benefiting from schemes to integrate them smoothly into the education system.

As pointed out by Mr. Vanbergen, the notion of equality of outcomes was taken very seriously by Spain. Compensatory programmes were seen to be an important instrument towards achieving it. The government had adopted an integrated social and economic policy for the rural areas and educational funding was accompanied by employment schemes. Promoting social mobility was highly desirable, but helping youngsters to attain an appropriate level of education was an end in itself, whatever their future beyond school. In 1983, a sub-directorate for Compensatory Education had been set up to coordinate schemes for drop-outs, the inhabitants of deprived rural and urban areas, and other disadvantaged target groups. Distance education programmes were being organised to assist educationally underprivileged groups. Adult education schemes for marginal groups were also run jointly with local authorities and firms.

A further series of measures had been introduced to improve the curriculum of basic education. Experiments were being carried out with different age groups to develop better adjusted programmes and to prepare for a longer period of compulsory education. Two options were being considered for reorganising the levels of compulsory schooling following its extension to age fifteen or sixteen. One possibility was a structure of six years plus four years, plus a year of vocational education for those who would leave the system or plus two years of post-compulsory education for those who would not. A second possibility, which was under consideration by the Ministry, was to establish an age eleven-to-fifteen cycle, giving five years of primary plus four years of lower secondary, plus one year of vocational training or plus three years of post-compulsory education. Experiments with pilot groups were already under way and would continue for some time.

The Swedish delegate wondered whether the compensatory programmes were delivered directly from the centre or whether the Autonomous Regions, perhaps better judges of local needs, had a part to play as well. *The Finnish delegate* wished to know what Spanish policy might be in relation to the danger of bringing an end to local cultural activity when small local schools were closed. *Mr. Gass* (OECD) asked whether certain schools could be developed in such a way as to promote local employment initiatives.

The Spanish delegation replied that the disappearance of small rural schools had indeed gone hand in hand with the impoverishment of communities both in cultural and economic terms. Drop-out rates were also higher among pupils who were obliged to travel long distances and leave home for lengthy periods of time. The Ministry of Education had therefore pursued a policy of maintaining rural schools despite the considerable expense entailed. As to the identification of zones for compensatory education, these were defined, with reference to the needs of small areas, by the Autonomous Regions under the supervision of the Ministry. Local surveys and specific indicators such as drop-out and unemployment rates were taken into account.

The French delegate wished to know what procedures the Spanish authorities intended to follow in order to standardize evaluation of what pupils learned at school. *The Danish delegate* wondered whether it might not be better to postpone the integration of handicapped children until the structural and curricular reforms had been accomplished because, in the meantime, teachers might not be able to spare them the attention and energy that would be called for. *The Australian delegate* was struck by the emphasis on equality of outcomes. Would the Minister elaborate on what this implied?

In answer to the question about handicapped children, *the Spanish delegation* explained that integration would be implemented over a period of eight years and would benefit from adequate funding. Compulsory schools with sixteen classes, for instance, would have two teachers specialised in therapeutical pedagogy, one specialist in speech handicaps and, if required, a trained teacher for children with motor handicaps. Public opinion had accepted this measure very positively.

As for the concept of equality of outcomes, basic general education must, by definition, provide a common fund of knowledge and understanding to each individual and citizen. Its function was not to select but to give each child an equal chance in life. Later on, after basic schooling, talent and experience at work would be able to play their differentiating role but each person must be allowed to go as far as he or she wished.

Mr. Carabaña took up the French question about standardization of evaluation and marking. Naturally, teachers must mark according to their own judgement. However, the State fixed standards and norms relating to what must be achieved and set the terms of reference against which teachers must undertake their assessment. In particular, marking had to be based on actual performance and not on an estimation of capacity to follow a particular course of study in the future.

III

THE SIXTEEN-TO-NINETEEN AGE GROUP

Question 12

It is difficult to define adequately the content and methods of the 11-16 curriculum and, more particularly, of the 14-16 curriculum, without having a clear conception of the purpose of the succeeding curriculum for 16-19 year-olds. For one thing, there is the problem of what to do for those who drop out during this cycle or who eventually leave school without a useful qualification. The existing dual model appears to reinforce the social inequalities in the system. Representatives of the trade unions and employers' associations informed the examiners that they were in favour of a comprehensive upper secondary school model. How do the authorities view this idea? In what ways is it intended to reorient and reorganise the 16-19 curriculum?

Question 13

What is to be the specific place of vocational training in the reform of secondary education (14-19)? The 14-16 cycle will offer five hours a week of "technology" but this will be of a general character. Would it not be preferable to offer diversified and specialised programmes of vocational training from the age of fifteen under the supervision of the Ministry of Labour or other ministries, institutions or enterprises – which presupposes a 5 + 4 + 3 rather than a 5 + 3 + 2 + 2 cycle – so as to shorten the time required to obtain a qualification and to enable those young people who are antagonized or bored by school to feel themselves adults at an earlier age? On the other hand, what will be the level of competence and specialisation to be obtained at the age of eighteen or nineteen, that is, how will vocational training be considered at the post-secondary level?

Question 14

As a rule, OECD examiners do not pose questions about discrete parts of the curriculum. However, in Spain they were struck by the apparently low priority given to education in the creative arts in curricular proposals for the reformed secondary school, all the more so in view of the country's unusually rich artistic heritage. Is it assumed that education in the creative arts should be mainly confined to specially designated institutions?

Mr. Frausto da Silva opened discussion on this controversial area by recalling that in the Background Report it was said that the upper secondary school (BUP) had distorted the idea of a formative secondary education which prepared for life as well as for higher education. He considered that the implications of these two types of preparation ought to be discussed by the Committee. Regarding FP1 and FP2, the vocational educational branch which was also required to provide an adequate general education, there were two different views. The general public considered them to be the poor man's second choice, while in the employers' estimation they were valueless in comparison with what they themselves had to offer in terms of experience and training. Thus, everyone, including the authorities, believed that change was necessary.

Mr. Frausto da Silva posed four main questions. Was it feasible to define a new fourteen-to-sixteen cycle without considering what would follow? Was it acceptable to maintain a system with two unequal tracks? Might it not be more advisable to have, first, a three-year comprehensive cycle for the fifteen to eighteen year-olds, and then vocational training outside the formal system of vocational education? Would it not be more economic and more appropriate to have a 5 + 4 + 3 year structure instead of a 5 + 3 + 2 + 2 (or + 3) one? As a final comment, given Spain's unique cultural heritage, why was there no mention of education in the creative arts in the Background Report?

The Spanish delegation underlined that, as yet, no structures had been determined. For the time being, it was not so much policies which were under discussion as plans. The structural problem was being approached with growing realism and it was recognised that it would be necessary to develop each cycle with reference to the other cycles. Vocational education was generally felt to be unsatisfactory and so demand was very high for the academic tracks.

The Minister intended that extended compulsory education should be one track and general, whereas post-compulsory education should provide semi-specialised training as well as general education. The objective was to avoid social discrimination through early selection and to give each person a broad and solid grounding for adult life. The employers' associations accepted this as did most trade unions. Experiments had begun with two further years of comprehensive education. It was clear that problems would come in the tenth year rather than in the ninth, since it was then that pupils would begin to be anxious to get outside and lead adult lives. This was why the 5 + 4 + 3 and the 6 + 4 + 2 options were being examined. So far nothing had been decided.

It had been proposed that there should be five or six tracks leading up to the high school diploma, with the following possible labels: Artistic; Languages; Natural Sciences; Human Sciences; Technical-Industrial; Technical-Administrative. All tracks would share a common element and specific options would permit specialisation as chosen by the student. At the end of the post-compulsory two-year cycle the authorities were considering introducing a new nationally recognised qualification, opening access either to higher education or to the world of work. This diploma would be equivalent to the existing specialist technician qualification, that is, level 3 according to the Common Market classification. Existing vocational education faculties would be used to provide this education.

The Minister agreed with Mr. Frausto da Silva that there was a danger both of curricula being unduly academic and of too many young people being drawn by the prestige of the tracks which led to university. Over the last fifteen years the university student population had already jumped from 70 000 to 700 000. It would be necessary to increase the attraction of vocational education. Specialising the post-compulsory tracks by incorporating existing high-quality professional training might provide a solution.

It was difficult to integrate the creative arts into the ordinary curriculum. Spain had many Applied Arts Schools (71) with more than 25 000 students. Their curricula have been partially renewed and improved. About 200 000 pupils attended music schools outside the official system. As just mentioned, an artistic track was to be one of the main five or six curricular options, but it was also the only one for which as yet no plan had been developed.

Regarding the universities, there were two important problem areas: the question of access and the need to reform the curriculum. In the present five-year system many drop-outs occurred in the first two years. With a three-year first cycle of general studies followed by a more specialised second cycle, there might be less wastage of talent and funds. As for access, the creation of a nationally recognised diploma would be a major step forward.

In relation to the plan for a nationally recognised qualification, *the New Zealand delegate* wondered whether there was not a risk that the system might become led by examinations. In addition, how much importance could be attached to the assessment of individual achievement? *The French delegate* asked whether the five or six main tracks, particularly the technical-industrial ones, would have many sub-tracks, so that genuine specialist vocational education could be provided? According to *Mr. Vanbergen*, adding to the more academic tracks several technical tracks, instead of just one, might attract more pupils.

Mr. Carabaña, in answer to the New Zealand delegate's question, said that the curriculum was, indeed, consciously designed not to be examination-led. On the other hand, a means of assessment, valid right across the country, was necessary. A commission of experts had been convened to address the problem but they were not finding it an easy task. The difficulty was compounded by the requirement to provide, concurrently, recognition of the skills and achievement of the youngsters who had not obtained any paper qualifications.

Mr. Segovia indicated that the five or six areas of education had been selected with the intention of giving each pupil a broad base of knowledge and understanding with common elements for students in each branch and options for specialisation. The system would thus be flexible, allowing many optional tracks as well as movement from one to another, and opening access both to university and to vocational education qualifications. It was vital, with whole industrial sectors changing, shrinking or disappearing, that students and trainees be as qualified and as flexible as possible. All the various organisations currently responsible for training, whether public or private, were involved in planning the reforms and it was intended that a system of combined on-and-off-the-job training would be set up for those who would choose not to go to university.

IV

TEACHERS AND THEIR TRAINING
AND POST-SECONDARY EDUCATION

Question 15

The far-reaching reform envisaged by the authorities will necessitate a fundamental overhaul of teacher training. What is the reaction of the Spanish authorities to the proposal that the same level of education and training should be offered to all teachers of all pupils from six to nineteen and even three to nineteen? Could this be so arranged as to arrive at a reasonable balance between specialisation by age groups (3-8; 8-11; 11-16; 16-18/19 or 3-6; 6-11; 11-16; 16-18/19) and specialisation according to subject disciplines? At the least, do they see a case for offering a common curriculum for all students including general pedagogy, educational psychology and social studies, complemented by special courses related to the teaching of specific age groups and subjects?

Question 16

Within recent years considerable efforts have been made to improve in-service training by such means as establishing university-based programmes, creating teaching and resource centres, and offering "distance" courses, and by relying upon the voluntary efforts of teachers' associations, financially supported by the authorities. Nevertheless, there are still many teachers who remain untouched by the new educational aims and methods. Is it intended, therefore, to consolidate and expand the existing arrangements, for example by setting up a systematic network of teaching resource centres? Will there be any attempt to encourage applied research in the institutes of education with a view to marrying theory and practice and responding to teachers' needs in the actual school context?

Question 17

Like many OECD countries Spain has experienced a massive expansion of higher education over a very short space of time with consequential pressures on teaching and material resources as well as a high rate of student wastage or drop-out during the initial years of study. What measures have been taken or are to be taken to sustain the very quality of higher education against the background of high enrolments?

Question 18

The period required to obtain a first degree and, where desired, a post-graduate degree, appears to be very long, especially in view of the existence of the one-year university preparatory course in the upper secondary schools (COU) and of the plan to institute a three-year upper secondary cycle? Do the authorities envisage any shortening of the period of university studies? For example, would they contemplate introducing a short-cycle degree of two or three years as already exists for Escuelas Universitarias?

Question 19

To mobilise a strong innovatory capacity in all fields, and notably in science and technology, is generally recognised to be of paramount importance for the economic strength of Spain, especially at the time of its accession to the European Economic Community. To what extent and by what means are the universities expected to contribute to the generation of that capacity? How do the authorities perceive the balance between the teaching and research functions of the universities?

As *Mr. Vanbergen* saw it, the problems of teacher training in Spain were not very different from those of other OECD countries. In placing responsibility in the hands of the universities, the structural weaknesses seemed to have been overcome but many questions remained unanswered. What weight should be given to one or another area of knowledge and how much stress should be laid on pedagogical training itself? Should such training concentrate on didactics or ought it to extend further into the study of educational problems in general? The authorities wished to create a unified teacher training system. This did not mean the same academic or pedagogical training for all, but training up to the same level which would increase mobility and perhaps make it easier, in the long term, to adjust the whole system. It appeared that mastery of a discipline had always been emphasized as the main criterion of aptitude. In the future, it was to be hoped that equal importance would be attached to pedagogical methods and that teachers would keep up-to-date with new developments in pedagogical theory and practice. Much was being done to improve in-service training, involving many bodies including the universities; the attempt to develop a diversified and coordinated system was, in this respect, very promising. It appeared to the examiners, however, that the training system as a whole still required more coordination; the precise role and responsibility of each institution needed to be defined more clearly.

The Spanish delegation stated that the national authorities were currently faced with a serious problem of oversupply of teachers. In no field, even in those where there were shortages in other countries, such as mathematics and technology, would there be any problem in recruiting enough staff. Moreover, 85 per cent of personnel were aged under forty-five and, given the demographical trend, demand for new teachers would be very low for some time to come. Therefore, efforts to raise the quality of teaching would have to be concentrated on in-service training.

A recent survey by the CIDE showed that a majority of teachers were satisfied with their training in terms of fields of study and content. Nevertheless, the authorities were conscious of weaknesses in the system. The teacher training network was not yet properly integrated into the higher education system and its institutions tended to be set apart from the universities to which they were supposed to be attached. Secondly, due to the complexity of the previous system, many teachers found themselves occupying posts other than those for which they were qualified, for example in language teaching. Actual reforms of training would have to be carried out by the universities themselves since they were now autonomous, the Minister being able to control only access to training and to posts in state schools. A Green Paper on reforming teacher training had just been published. This was, basically, a proposal to the Universities Council that teacher training be properly integrated. If higher education was to be reorganised into cycles, then the training for basic school teachers should correspond, for instance, to a first-level degree, and secondary-school teacher training should fit in somewhere in relation to the first two cycles. Pedagogy should be taught by education departments whereas the appropriate university faculties would be responsible for teaching special subjects. It would be necessary also to find a way of including a year of practical teacher training within university course requirements.

In-service training was being reformed in various ways. A new network of institutions was being established, which would provide training near to the schools where teachers were located. In the past, training centres had tended to be inaccessible to teachers in large cities and even more so to those from rural areas. By 1986-87 there would be approximately 200 such training centres, catering for about 900 teachers at a time and working in collaboration with the 440 centres responsible for compensatory education. They would thus be able to prepare staff for the reforms to come, for example in relation to the raising of overall standards, the integration of handicapped children, and the introduction of computer sciences into the curriculum.

There was also an ambitious programme for training teachers. In 1985-86, 1 850 people would be attending courses. This was essential for the implementation of plans to overcome shortages in the teaching of physical education, music, arts, languages and pre-school education. Financial support for the activities of the teachers' federations, such as summer schools, had also been increased. A number of agreements had been signed with the universities for the training of special education staff. For instance, the autonomous University of Madrid organised courses and seminars for specialists in dealing with children with mental and physical handicaps and linguistic deficiencies. Coordination of all these services so as to make them as effective as possible was a major priority for the Ministry of Education and Science.

On higher education, *Mr. Milutinović* indicated that, as many of the examiners' recommendations had already been taken on board, they would like the Spanish delegation to answer three questions in particular. In relation to the universities, was it yet possible to evaluate the success of the new departments and the newly established councils? Secondly, how were the universities coping with the process of restructuring? Fifty per cent of the student population studied the humanities. Would it be possible to move around all the university teachers so that they covered the new curricula in every discipline in every university department? The graft of the teacher training colleges on the universities had not taken well. Attempts to break down the traditional five-year degree courses appeared artificial; yet five years was a long time to study for a first degree and surely the cost to the State must be prohibitive. Finally, there was a big gap between research inside the universities and outside. Could the delegation explain how it was intended to bridge the gulf between industrial and non-industrial research?

Mr. Lamo de Espinosa replied that it was not yet possible to give positive answers to all Mr. Milutinović's questions as many matters were still being discussed by the Ministry and the university authorities. Perhaps the most important point was that central governments and the Autonomous Regions had conceded full autonomy to the universities. These were now undertaking their own reorganisation into departments where staff with similar interests and research backgrounds would be regrouped, so that each would be free to work and teach in his or her own chosen field. Some of the older foundations might find it easier to respect traditional patterns in redesigning their faculties, but some more recent institutions were already fully implementing the departmental model. Regrouping would make it possible, for the first time, for Spanish universities to organise proper post-graduate degree courses.

Naturally, research would also benefit enormously from this more efficient use of human resources.

The new organisation would also fit in with the redesign of degree courses into shorter cycles. This was considered essential in order that higher education might be opened up to a greater number of Spaniards. Falling rolls would also make it easier to offer courses to a larger range of people. In the meantime, capacity was excessive in some areas and limited in others. Without encouraging dramatic changes the State authorities had permitted increases of resources in some cases, while the universities had the right to refuse entry on the grounds of inability to provide adequate tuition. In general, despite the rapid increase in the student population over recent years, it had been possible to expand capacity quite adequately and quality seemed actually to have been enhanced. It was hoped that the new shorter-cycle degrees would bring further improvements in quality and that, accompanied by a more relevant curriculum and a better student/teacher ratio, they would see fewer drop-outs in the first few years than under the previous system. Quality and national recognition of the new degrees and cycles would be monitored by the new Universities Council, which would set standards and norms, including a minimum of thirty per cent compulsory studies for each curriculum.

In his closing remarks, *the Minister* emphasized that it was scarcely possible to come to detailed conclusions about a series of reforms which had so many diverse aspects and which, moreover, was still being implemented. As Flaubert had put it "To want to draw conclusions is inept" (*L'ineptie, c'est de vouloir conclure*).

The main desideratum was to set the right national policies. First, it was essential to offer secondary-school provision that was more and more stimulating. Fighting youth unemployment meant not only a labour policy but also ambitious reforms in secondary education. Next, university students required an education adapted to their real needs and the needs of a modern society. The thrust of reform had been towards meeting these two objectives. The examiners' report and the day's debate had been very enlightening. The relationship between Spain and the OECD Education Committee was going through a most fruitful phase.

Mr. Frausto da Silva said that, despite the great diversity of origins, cultures and languages which typified Spain, the examiners had been struck, in the course of their evaluation of the reforms, by the strong will of people in all walks of life to achieve progress, to modernise institutions and to consolidate freedom and democracy.

Part Three

THE SPANISH EDUCATION SYSTEM

Summary of the Background Report prepared
by the Centro Nacional de Investigación y Documentación Educativa, CIDE,
Madrid, 1985

SUMMARY OF THE BACKGROUND REPORT

1. MODERN SPAIN:
THE ADMINISTRATIVE BACKGROUND TO EDUCATION

In order to explain the education system and government policy, it is necessary, first, to give an account of the social and economic situation in Spain, the administrative organisation of education (very much caught up in the recent political changes) and the sources and level of educational funding.

Social, economic and political context

According to the 1981 Census, Spain has an average density of population of 75 inhabitants per sq. km. This population, however, is distributed unevenly; the coastal areas have a higher density than the hinterland, with the exception of Madrid. More than half of Spain's population (55 per cent) is distributed around four Autonomous Regions: Andalucia, Catalonia, Madrid and Valencia. The remaining 45 per cent are distributed among 14 other Autonomous Regions.

The size of the workforce in Spain has always tended to be relatively low, compared with that in other OECD countries. Far from levelling out, this trend has in fact increased over the period covered by the last four censuses. There are many causes for this, the more obvious being the generalisation of schooling, the lowering of the retirement age, and the raising from 14 to 16 of the legal age for starting work; these figures have offset the rise in the number of women in employment.

In 1984 the workforce was distributed as follows among the economic sectors: 18.2 per cent in agriculture, 35.2 per cent in industry and construction and 46.6 per cent in services and other types of work. This distribution represents a great transformation since 1940, when 50 per cent of the population was employed in the agricultural sector.

Despite the drop in the size of the workforce the number of people unable to find work has been growing steadily over recent years, since, in absolute terms, available work has been shrinking. Thus, of all the countries in the OECD, Spain is the one with the lowest proportion of people in work. The total population ratio of people in employment or out is 3.34, higher even than Turkey (3.11) and Ireland (3.03), and almost double that of Sweden (1.97), Japan (2.10) or Denmark (2.16). Even when these ratios are corrected by taking into account the very small share of part-time work and also the black economy, the statistics hardly change. At the present time, the rate of unemployment is one of the highest in the OECD area, at about 20 per cent.

Not surprisingly, the rate of unemployment is higher among young people, and although the number of working youngsters has fallen through the raising of the school-leaving age, the figures for youth unemployment are still around 50 per cent. Unemployment is the most serious problem faced by the Spanish economy, whose capacity for creating jobs was small even in the years of most rapid growth.

The 1981 census produced the following figures concerning educational attainment in Spain: illiterates, 7.92 per cent; no schooling or incomplete schooling, 23.05 per cent; those with primary education, 42.42 per cent, those with secondary education, 19.53 per cent, university students 6.68 per cent. This breakdown varies greatly according to age groups: thus, while among people over 65 about 50 per cent are illiterates or barely able to read, in the under-25 group, 50 per cent have secondary education.

In 1982, with respect to current prices and exchange rates, the average *per-capita income* was US$ 4 788, approximately half that of France (9 961) and one-third that of Switzerland (14 929). When relative and price indexes are taken into account the income per capita was US$ 6 870, compared with 10 747 in France and 13 106 in the United States. In real terms, therefore, the situation was better than in nominal terms, and real disposable income was about half that of the United States. The per-capita income was low given the level of technology but consumer capacity is relatively higher as public expenditure is much lower than in other countries. Disposable income is unevenly distributed among families, by European standards, and there is no tendency for it to even out.

From the *political* point of view, Spain is a parliamentary monarchy. In November 1975 General Franco died and was replaced as Head of State by the King. From then on began a process of excision – led from within – of the institutions which had upheld his régime. The Franco *Cortes* passed by a large majority a Political Reform Act which made it possible to hold in 1977 the first free elections since 1936, and to dismantle the most characteristic institutions of Franco's government, such as the "Vertical" trade unions and the organisation called the "Movement". Votes in the election were largely cast for those political groups which represented the moderate tendencies of left or right, the UCD (Democratic Union of the Centre) and the PSOE (the Workers' Socialist Party of Spain), leaving in a definite minority the more extreme conservatives of the *Alianza Popular* (Popular Alliance) and the Communist Party. The distribution of votes and seats at the 1977 election gave a majority to the UCD, which was to govern until 1982. The parliament elected in 1977 devised a Constitution which was passed by referendum in 1978. The transition from dictatorship to democracy took place with remarkably little trouble.

As far as educational policy is concerned, the two most influential factors have been limited growth in its share of the budget, not enough to carry through swiftly all the reforms outlined in the government's programme, and the fact that, on finishing his studies, at whatever level, the only outlook for the young person is a long period of searching for employment.

The administrative framework of education

The Constitution of 1978 recognises that the Spanish nation has a great diversity of communities and regions, each of which has the right to a degree of self-government. Administrative structures are therefore being reformed to conform with the territorial reorganisation of the country and redistribution of political power between the State and the Autonomous Regions.

Within ministerial departments and the other national organs which make up the central administration, the whole structure of decision-making as such is slowly being phased out and replaced by coordination, planning, inspection and documentation services, these being the functions that will henceforth be assumed by the central authorities under the new decentralised order.

The Ministry of Education and Science has adapted to the process of decentralisation in the belief that education is a responsibility which must be shared, some aspects being the prerogative of the State, and others, of the Autonomous Regions. Many functions and educational services have already been transferred to four Autonomous Regions and the transfer to another two is in preparation. Once the process of political decentralisation in the educational field has been completed by the transfer of powers to the other eleven Autonomous Regions further reforms will be implemented within the Ministry itself.

National educational policy is determined by the Minister, assisted by an advisory council, made up of the Secretary of State for Universities and Research, two under-secretaries, the Chairman of the Higher Council for Scientific Research, the Executive Secretary-General, the several Directors General controlling departments, the Director of the Minister's advisory team and the Director of the Secretary of State's advisory team.

Reserving certain powers to the State will guarantee the basic unity of the education system throughout the country. This concept of "basic unity" leaves the door open for the Autonomous Regions to exercise their own powers so as to complement the basic system with distinctive contributions of their own as considered appropriate. The areas reserved to the State are:

a) Regulation of academic and professional qualifications so as to ensure equal validity throughout the country.

b) Institution of minimum standards in application of Article 27 of the Constitution which establishes basic rights to education.

c) Determining general structure of the education system, including: fixing the period of compulsory schooling; regulating levels, grades, specialist fields, cycles and modes of teaching; specifying the availability of different courses at different levels; specifying the requirements for access from one level of education to another.

d) Establishing basic education throughout the country, that is, the compulsory provision of a common body of knowledge and authorisation of the appropriate manuals or textbooks.

e) Determining certain minimal requirements for schools and centres of learning, with reference to the academic qualifications of the teachers, teacher/pupil ratios, teaching and sporting facilities and installations, and the number of school places available.

f) In those Autonomous Regions which have their own language (Catalonia, the Basque Country, Galicia, Valencia and the Balearic Islands), the State also has the power to guarantee the right to learn Castilian.

Those matters for which responsibility is not attributed to the State by the Constitution will be the concern of the *Autonomous Regions* by virtue of their respective statutes.

In fact, the Autonomous Regions have already assumed almost all their powers as laid down in their respective statutes. This means that there is now an educational administrative body in each of the Regions, which is adequately structured, and which has sufficient resources to carry out its appropriate functions. These resources are for the most part either inherited from the previous state administration or handed down through transfers on the basis of agreements between the central administration and the Autonomous Regions.

Finally, it should be said that there do exist areas for which neither the central administration nor the Autonomous Regions take full responsibility and which require the cooperation of both. These *shared responsibilities* are the following:

a) Exchange of information necessary for overall planning in the field of education and the best use of available resources.

b) Educational research.

c) In-service training of teachers.

d) Distance education, which is provided by three national public centres and a large number of private ones.

The coexistence of various different public administrations at different levels, as a result of political decentralisation, requires co-ordination to ensure the proper functioning of institutional machinery. To this end *Sectoral Conferences* have been set up, on which sit the Directors of Education of the various Autonomous Regions and the Minister of Education, who acts as chairman.

In addition, observance of the laws regulating the powers described above is assured through a "Higher Inspectorate", which has the task of overseeing basic education, the general management of the education system, academic qualifications, the format of attendance registers and the basic conditions guaranteeing the equality of all Spanish people in relation to linguistic rights, subsidies and grants; it is also responsible for processing information and preparing statistics for the national authorities. This new monitoring instrument works alongside others in existence since 1970: the Technical Inspectorate (which has a specific role in the field of education), and the General Inspectorate of Services, which watches over administrative procedures and resource management.

Financing of education

It is a commonplace to point to the low level of educational spending in Spain, which, in 1981, was just 5 per cent of GNP. However, this percentage is not entirely accurate, as it does not include the expenditures of certain public institutions outside the scope of the Ministry of Education and Science; nor does it take into account private expenditure on student maintenance and support.

In recent years, the Ministry's share in the general state budget has been 15 per cent, or 2.7 per cent of GNP. Comparison with other OECD countries shows Spain in an unfavourable light. Thus, while in 1979 the Ministry's budget equalled 2.3 per cent of GNP, in Germany it was 4.6 per cent, in Australia 5.9 pour cent, in Canada 7.4 per cent and in France 3.7 per cent. The only countries less highly placed were Greece, Portugal and Turkey. However, the Ministry is not the only recipient of public expenditure. Other departments, as well as the Autonomous Regions and the local municipalities, contribute substantially to the public costs of education. As a result, in 1983, expenditure amounted not to the 631 000 million pesetas of the Ministerial budget, but to 804 000 million, about 3.5 per cent of GNP, a percentage roughly equal to that of France.

In addition, it is necessary to bear in mind the low level of Spain's public spending in general. The Ministerial budget has, in fact, much the same share of the general state budget as in any other OECD country. The general state budget, taken as a whole, makes up a much smaller percentage of GNP than in any other OECD country. The low level of public spending in Spain, therefore, is not at the level of central, but of local administration. The educational budget is 15 per cent of the state budget, but public spending on education is only 10 per cent of total public expenditure. Of course this is a very low figure and it is in fact made up by private contributions to their children's education from families, who thus play a very important part in the financing of education. Nevertheless, the rate of growth of private expenditure on education has been less than that of public expenditure, as can be seen from the fact that in 1970 the ratio between the two was 70:100 whereas in 1981 it was 45:100.

The pattern of public and private spending on education is quite complicated. Not all private spending goes on private education and not all public spending goes on state education. Families pay matriculation fees and other contributions to state education, while the State subsidises private education and gives grants to individual students.

The degree to which private individuals ought to finance state education and to which the State ought to finance private education is the subject of constant controversy. With respect to compulsory schooling, the Constitution lays down that the public authorities must assist those private schools which comply with legal requirements; moreover, it stipulates that compulsory education must be free to all young people. Consequently, the legal assessment of the sums to be allocated to subsidies, and the conditions which have to be fulfilled by schools before they receive funds, have become the subject of quite a battle between political parties, trade unions, pressure groups and others with strong views on the subject.

Since 1970, the one item of the *Ministerial budget* which has grown at a sustained rate has been transfers, to the detriment of real investment. The percentage devoted to the running of the state schools (personnel and services) has remained more or less stable at around 58 per cent; however, real investment has dropped from 31.6 to 12.3 per cent, whereas transfers, which were 8.7 per cent in 1970 stood at 30.9 per cent by 1984.

The greater part of these financial transfers are devoted to subsidising private education, to grants and to school transport. The rate of increase in subsidies to private schools is approximately 15 per cent per annum, so that, from 1973 onwards, more than 90 per cent of private schools offering compulsory education have been subsidised, whereas previously, under the dictatorship, these schools did not receive any subsidies at all. This reflects a choice made in relation to the financing of education by successive governments since 1975. In order to guarantee free education, they could have resorted to the all-out development of state provision. In fact, it was not until 1978 that state education was given a real boost, as a result of pressure from the Opposition. Until then, it was thought a better idea to guarantee free education by means of subsidies to private schools, thus saving on the cost of building state schools.

Some *private expenditure* may be considered as compensation for inadequate public funding. However, some may be regarded as a complement to public expenditure, since families, in proportion to their incomes, tend to spend money on education even when the public authorities guarantee free school places of equal quality. So, expenditure on education increases in relation to family income because money is spent on extra-curricular activities such as transport, school meals and child care at non-compulsory educational levels, and the level is usually roughly equal to what parents save on normal school fees as a result of subsidies.

2. THE SPANISH EDUCATION SYSTEM: STRUCTURE AND GENERAL CHARACTERISTICS

The present education system dates from the General Education Act of 1970, which for the first time in this century laid down regulations and structured the entire education system. It has a very wide scope and attempts to overcome all the internal contradictions into which the system had fallen as a result of a succession of partial reforms, which had been insufficient to respond to the acceleration of social and economic change in Spain at the time. The terms of the Act are based on the liberal educational tradition and implicitly recognise the failure of the authoritarian type of education which was typical of the national Catholicism of the preceding thirty years.

With regard to general structure, the system established by this Act is still in force, though, as might be expected, during the fifteen years since it came into force gradual implementation of its terms has been accompanied by certain reforms. In particular, the change of political régime required by the Constitution of 1978 has, logically enough, entailed some differences of approach and partial modifications.

Structure of the education system

Within the overall perspective of lifelong education, the General Education Act (LGE) established a unitary system (the double tracks which existed in the primary and lower secondary sectors prior to the LGE were abolished) which was also flexible (many "bridges" and opportunities for hopping from one branch to another at the higher levels were created), with the aim of giving the entire population equality of opportunity in education, and the chance to develop their maximum potential. Thus, the system has a four-tier structure with, in addition, provision for lifelong education for adults:

a) *Pre-school*, which is included for the first time in the school system, though it is neither compulsory nor free.

b) *Basic General Education* (EGB, *Educación General Básica*) compulsory and free schooling covering the period between the ages of 6 and 14, and which is divided into two stages equivalent to the primary and lower secondary of other countries.

c) *Post-compulsory Secondary Education* (*Enseñanzas Medias*) (equivalent to upper secondary in other countries) which comprises the *Bachillerato Unificado Polivalente* (BUP) and the University Orientation Course (COU, *Curso de Orientación Universitaria*) on the one hand, and Vocational Training (*Formación Profesional*, FP) on the other, the first level of which is also compulsory for those who are not doing the *Bachillerato*.

d) *University education*, which is divided into three cycles,

Characteristics of the education system

Our intention here is to sketch briefly a broad picture of the Spanish education system, as it has developed under the General Education Act of 1970, stressing what has really happened and leaving aside elements which, in practice, it has not been possible to develop.

• The most important achievement is without any doubt the *generalisation* of education from 6 to 14 years for the whole population. This means generalisation in two senses of the word: the integration into one non-discriminatory system of all children in the age group and full schooling for all. In fact, enrolment has increased from 64 per cent of the 6-10 year-olds, and 34 per cent of 11-14 year olds, in 1968, to practically 100 per cent since 1975.

• A feature of the Spanish reform of 1970 was its concern with the *quality* of education. The General Education Act not only provided for the extension of education to all but specified that it must be an education of quality. So, curricular reform, both of content and method, was undertaken and a great effort was made to improve school facilities, teaching materials, the training of teachers and so forth. (It was for this reason that Teacher Training for Basic General Education was incorporated into the universities.) It cannot be said that we have yet reached the desired level of quality, but it can be said that considerable improvements have been made in relation to the past, at least in Basic General Education. Naturally there are areas which are still deficient: one-teacher schools, bad schooling conditions, the huge problem caused by the fact that pre-school education is not free, and much to do in terms of renewing curricular content and pedagogical methods. But, from a historical perspective, one must recognise that much progress was made in the 1970s in relation to those authoritarian schools, so unconcerned about the technical and pedagogical aspects of teaching, which existed at the end of the Civil War.

• The General Education Act brought an end to the pre-1970 notion that the State should play only a subsidiary role in education. In the preamble to the Act, the educational *function of the State* is recognised, in terms of responsibilities in the planning of education and the provision of school places. Planning at national, provincial and local level was initiated on the basis of a school map (*carte scolaire*) which showed the geographical distribution of schools and of studies which enabled the educational needs of the immediate future to be determined.

• Despite the role of the State as a public service in planning and controlling education, a characteristic of the Spanish system is the major place of *private education* at non-university levels. The proportion of state and private education at the various levels in the 1981-82 academic year was:

- at pre-school level 56.1 per cent state, 43.9 per cent private;
- Basic General Education, 63.5 per cent and 36.5 per cent respectively;
- Vocational Training, 55.9 per cent and 44.1 per cent, and
- *Bachillerato*, 66 per cent and 34 per cent.

In the last decade private education has lost ground in comparison with state education, but it still constitutes a major part of the system.

This dichotomy between state education and private education, particularly the problem of financing the latter, is one of the points which is most ambiguously treated by the General Education Act and has given rise to several problems in recent years. Naturally, the tensions caused have arisen not only for economic reasons, but also for ideological ones. We shall leave these aside, however. It is nonetheless evident that the existence of such a large private education sector constitutes a peculiarity in the system from the pedagogical point of view, if only in terms of the scope and variety that it offers. Thus, in state schools, a pupil can expect average standards of acceptable quality within certain moderately variable parameters to which there are few exceptions. But pupils in private schools may experience very diverse quality, running from tiny institutions of low quality, with poor equipment and hardly any resources, to spacious, modern, comfortable and even luxurious establishments; from institutions which are highly traditional in their concept of education to others which are innovatory or display progressive tendencies; from schools with a close dependence on the Catholic Church to others covering a wide range of ideologies or eschewing ideology altogether. In any event, this wide variety is an important factor to be borne in mind when it comes to understanding and judging the system. Furthermore, the private schools give rise to another peculiarity: large-scale transport requirements for schoolchildren in the big cities since children may attend a school not in the area where they live but at some considerable distance from their homes. This need for transportation, when added to existing transport needs in rural areas, reaches a considerable volume, and in some cases it almost comes to the point where there is a "para-school" problem.

• It might also be said that the Spanish system is structurally *not very selective* in comparison with those of other countries. This was in fact a principle of the General Education Act by virtue of which a system of continuous assessment was established. This means that, apart from certain techniques of measuring pupils' performance built into the dynamics of the classroom, there are no examinations outside the process of the pupils' learning, that is, no examinations administered by the State, the inspectorate or the local authorities, nor any body external to the actual centre of learning. There are no examinations to control passage from one level to the next, not even from primary to secondary education. Although it is true that there is a two-tier qualification at the end of Basic General Education (one which permits the pupils to go on to *Bachillerato* courses and the other which does not) which could be considered, and indeed often is, as a kind of selective screen. Even so, the Spanish system is still one of the least selective, particularly in comparison with those which hold an examination at the point of passage between primary and secondary education. In Spain, the *Graduado Escolar* diploma (which opens access to the *Bachillerato*) is obtained by 65 per cent of pupils who finish Basic General Education. Another factor is that, subsequently, pupils who could go on with secondary studies do not do so or drop out halfway through for social or economic reasons.

However, there does exist in Spain a selective examination for access to university. This, however, is an examination which practically all students who sit for it eventually pass and only certain degree courses which have a "numerus clausus" are truly competitive.

• One preoccupation of the educational reform of 1970 was to establish a relationship *between the education system and the world of employment*, in the sense that education should be a preparation for work and that movement between the two should always remain open. As a result of this, vocational training was incorporated into the education system, and an attempt was made to establish links with the world of work. Of the four possible ways of introducing vocational education in Spain the one known as "distancing" was chosen, that is, training carried out within the school system and obeying its rules, without being properly subject to the needs of the production system or labour-market structures. In a period of expansion, this system produces good results, but in the current period of economic crisis with accompanying unemployment, it creates large discrepancies between the world of education and that of employment.

However, at the other educational levels (Basic General Education, *Bachillerato* courses and University), the lack of links with the world of employment is almost total. There is nothing in the nature of "sandwich courses"; on-site practical training is limited to certain university courses; school visits to companies and service industries are very infrequent; career guidance does not exist in any institutionalised form; pre-technological training occupies an extremely secondary place in the curricula at all levels. Nonetheless, some progress has been made in this area since 1970 and, despite the fact that the times are not particularly propitious, a relationship between the education system and the labour market continues to be one of our goals.

• One of the most frequent criticisms of the 1970 reform has been that it is *not very democratic* in design, and is very *centralist* in the way in which it has been implemented.

The General Education Act and its subsequent development in study programmmes and methodological orientation was conceived by a group of experts who consulted, according to procedures rather more formal than real, certain social groups, but without reference to the people actually involved in the domain of education. This, in Spain, was to be expected, because of the very special political situation. But it must be pointed out that, in 1970, in relation to the conception of participation in educational planning, Spain was no great exception to the rest of the world.

Centralism – and its consequence, uniformity – continued to be a feature of the Spanish education system after 1970, despite the declarations of intention in the General Education Act. Control, planning, academic organisation in all its detail – all this has been centralised in the Ministry of Education, with little margin for decision-making being left to local communities and teaching centres. Both themes, decentralisation and participation in educational planning, have been much debated since the 1978 Constitution.

The Constitution of 1978 and its impact on the education system

Article 27 of the Constitution sets forth the general *principles* of all legislation concerning educational matters:

1. Everyone has the right to education. Freedom of choice of school is recognised.
2. The object of education is the full development of the human personality and respect for the democratic principle of social coexistence and basic rights and freedoms.
3. The public authorities guarantee the right of parents to ensurethat their children shall receive a moral and religious education which is in accordance with their own convictions.
4. Basic education is free and compulsory.
5. The public authorities guarantee the right of all to education, through the general planning of education with the effective participation of all sectors affected by it, and the creation of appropriate educational institutions.
6. Individuals and corporate bodies are recognised as having the freedom to set up institutions of learning, provided the principles set forth in the Constitution be respected.
7. Teachers, parents and, where applicable, students, shall participate in the control and management of centres set up by the State with public funds, according to terms established by law.
8. The public authorities shall inspect and standardize the education system in order to guarantee observance of the law.
9. The public authorities shall provide assistance to those educational institutions which meet the requirements of the law.
10. The autonomy of universities is recognised, according to terms to be established by law.

In order to establish the principles and rights set forth in this Article, two Organic Laws have been passed, and a third is awaiting a ruling following an appeal to the Constitutional Tribunal. Organic Law 5/1980 dated 19 June, which regulated the Schools Statute (*LOECE*), has as its objective the development of items 3 to 9 of Article 27 (the first two items may be regarded as permanent general guidelines). The Right to Education Act (*LODE*) passed by the plenary session of the *Congreso de Diputados* (Parliament) on 15 March 1984 will come into effect when the Constitutional Tribunal rules on the constitutional nature of certain of its clauses; it covers the same topics, and will replace the first, once it comes into force. The two regulate both state and private education at non-university level, but each one from a different political and ideological viewpoint (as might be expected, since they are the work of two different political parties). Each of the two laws basically establishes a framework for the relationship between the public authorities and private rights, and between the public sector and the private sector with regard to education, and regulates democratic participation in this field. However, first, whereas the *LOECE* does not deal with the important aspect of finance for private education at compulsory levels (which is being expressly left for a later Act), the *LODE* does so in detail; and secondly, the *LOECE* only regulates the participation of the educational community in the actual schools, whereas the *LODE* also points out the path to follow towards the generalisation of participation in education.

Item 10 of Article 27 is developed in the Organic Law (11/1983 dated 25 August) on University Reform, the purpose of which is to realise the long-held desire for university autonomy, which had already been expressed in the General Education Act.

The Constitution has also affected the education system in two other important respects. First is the *decentralisation* of educational administration, with the consequent transfer of powers and functions to the Autonomous Regions, and all that this implies in terms of erosion of uniformity in the system, though not in unity, which is maintained.

Secondly, the teaching of and in *vernacular languages* in Autonomous Regions with languages other than Castilian Spanish. Article 3 of the Constitution has this to say about the different languages in Spain:

1. Castilian is the official Spanish language of the State. All Spaniards have a duty to understand and the right to use it.
2. The other Spanish languages will also be official languages in the respective Autonomous Regions, in accordance with their statutes.
3. The richness of different linguistic forms is a part of the Spanish cultural heritage, which shall be the object of special respect and protection.

Thus, the Spanish State, as such, is monolingual, but "territorial bilingualism" exists in those communities where another language is also spoken, namely, the Balearic Islands, Catalonia, Galicia, the Basque Country and Valencia. In these communities, teaching of the local language has been ordained through five decrees, one for each region and several further edicts which extend them, regulating both their use as the working language in educational institutions and the teaching of them as a second language. The reason for choosing this territorial formula lies in the low proportion of linguistic minorities across regions. But the existence of numerous Castilian-speaking minorities in the Autonomous Regions does require protection for the teaching of the official language of the State.

3. CHARACTERISTICS AND ORGANISATION OF THE DIFFERENT EDUCATIONAL LEVELS

Pre-school

The General Education Act of 1970 recognises that, within the structure of the Spanish education system, pre-school education is the first stage of lifelong education for the individual. The fundamental objective is the harmonious development of the child's personality; it is not compulsory education and covers children up to the age of five. It is divided into two stages:

Kindergarten, for children of 2 and 3.
Nursery schools, for children of 4 and 5.

The educational content of these levels consists of games, language activities including, where appropriate, the mother tongue, rhythmic and plastic expression, observation of nature, logical and pre-numerical exercises, and the development of the sense of community.

At present, the characteristic which best defines pre-school education in Spain is "diversity". There are many different types of schools, whose character depends on the agency which manages them, the economic system which maintains them, and the child population which uses them. One attempt to classify them could be as follows:

- Pre-school units in state schools where EGB is also taught,
- Pre-school units in private EGB schools,
- Workers' Infant Schools, financed by the Ministry of Labour to assist the working mother,

- Infant Schools belonging to the National Institute for Social Assistance, established to take care of those children whose family conditions make it advisable that they receive extra attention,
- Company Infant Schools: institutions forming part of the enterprises where parents work,
- Municipal Infant Schools,
- Private Infant Schools.

During the academic year 1982-83, 1 187 617 children underwent pre-school education, that is approximately 50 per cent of the 2-5 year-old population. Distribution between the two sectors is as follows; 57.5 per cent of the total in state schools and 42.5 per cent in private schools.

The situation varies considerably between kindergartens, to which only 10 per cent of the 2-3 year-old population go, and nursery schools, which are attended by 85 per cent of children of 4 and 5 years of age. Furthermore, in kindergartens the private sector accounts for 87.7 per cent of pupils, with the other 12.3 per cent being in the state sector, whereas the situation in nursery schools is that 62 per cent of pupils go to state schools and 37.5 per cent to private ones.

The teaching staff caring for these children is as diversified as the schools themselves. The teachers in those schools which also teach Basic General Education have EGB teacher qualifications (awarded by the University Schools for the Training of Teachers), and in 33 per cent of these they are, in addition, specialists in pre-school education. But the teachers in the kindergartens, and especially in the private ones, have quite varied qualifications, often none at all. Faced with this varied situation, which has been brought about by the lack of any sectoral legislation and which is prejudicial to quality, an Infant Schools' Bill has been tabled in which standards and the regulation of the education of children of five and under will be established.

Basic General Education (EGB)

Basic General Education is that period of compulsory and unified education which all children undergo between the ages of 6 and 14. At the end of EGB, those pupils who have satisfactorily completed the 8 grades receive the diploma of *Graduado Escolar*. Those others, however, who have completed the eight years of schooling between the ages of 6 and 14, whether these eight years correspond to the 8 grades of EGB or not, and who have not reached the required academic standards, receive the *Certificado do Escolaridad*. There is also an opportunity to obtain the qualification of *Graduado Escolar* by passing satisfactorily an examination or test of maturity, which is open to people who have never been to EGB courses, or simply do not have the diploma.

The *Certificado de Escolaridad* is valid only for entry to vocational education schools of the first grade level, and for taking up not very specialised jobs. With the diploma of *Graduado Escolar*, however, the pupils may go on to prepare for the *Bachillerato*, and it is also a requisite for other jobs requiring a minimal qualification.

Academic organisation of EGB: curriculum, pedagogical methods and teachers

An educational level of this kind, which is unitary, compulsory and complete in itself in that it does not presuppose any kind of continuation, must of necessity have very special characteristics, given that it must be flexible enough to accommodate children with very different origins, from very different economic and social backgrounds and geographical areas, and provide a broad education which is a preparation for life itself and further studies. One thing that typifies EGB is the ascendancy of educational values over the learning of facts, and the attempt to cater both to the individual aspect of the human being (the development of the potentialities of each child) and to the social aspect (the acquisition of social habits and a feeling of belonging to a community). These principles imply a special practical approach to content, methods, teaching materials, school organisation and the pupil-teacher relationship.

The 1970 General Education Act divided the 8 years of study into two stages or cycles:

a) The first cycle covers five years (from 6 to 10 years of age, approximately), and gives a general inclusive type of education, which is taught by just one teacher. Rote-learning is totally subordinated to educational development which is perceived as awakening the intellectual faculties, facilitating social integration and stimulating the creative initiative of the pupil. Consequently, priority is given to instrumental techniques and the encouragement of all forms of expression (oral, written, body, plastic and so forth).

b) The second cycle covers three years (usually from 11 to 14). In this, a diversification by subjects and areas of knowledge, taught by several teachers, begins and greater importance is attached to the acquisition and organisation of knowledge, although techniques of expression continue to be seen as fundamental. Guidance is considered to be a key factor at this stage, in order to help the pupil to give some cohesion to his or her now diversified formative experiences, and to help cope with the options that will be open to him or her after the period of compulsory education.

The curriculum proposed by the Ministry for both stages was innovatory, in the sense that instead of a set of rigid norms that had to be observed willy-nilly, there were a certain number of directives and guidelines concerning teaching. Certain general objectives were stated as well as specific aims in relation to areas of knowledge and content and activities designed to achieve them.

This system led, of course, to deep-seated reform both of schools and teaching methods, and in some areas it caused a great deal of confusion, and was even considered to be the reason for some pupil failures. Because of this and the political decentralisation which obliges the State to establish minimal common bases for the education system, a new set of regulations for EGB was established in 1981.

The first stage of EGB was organised, for purposes of evaluation and in the interests of pupils, into two cycles:

a) The initial cycle, covering the first and second years of EGB,
b) The middle cycle, covering the third, fourth and fifth years of EGB.

For each cycle and for each year, certain "basic levels of reference" or minimum content were established, which the pupils had to attain before passing on to the next course or leaving school. This would avoid the risk of the programmes lacking definition, and would also make it possible to monitor pupils' performance, as well as that of teachers, schools and the education system itself. Special emphasis has been laid on unifying the common basic training for all Spanish children, which guarantees that diplomas at this level are compatible, alongside the cultivation of the appropriate cultural values of each region.

The present *curriculum* of the initial and middle cycles is as follows:

Area of study	Hours per week	
	Initial cycle	Middle cycle
Language	7	7
Mathematics	5	5
Social Sciences and Civic Education	} 5	2.5
Physical/Natural Sciences		3
Religion or Ethics	1.5	1.5
Artistic Education (Music, Painting, Drama)	3	2
Physical Education	2.5	3
Free options	1	1
	25	25

The second stage of EGB is to be named the Upper Cycle, but its reform is still being developed. Thus, the "pedagogical guidelines" of the General Education Act of 1970 are still in force at this level. The curriculum is made up of the following subjects (with a total of 25 teaching hours per week):

Spanish
A foreign language
Mathematics
Cultural and social studies/a sub-area of Civic Education
Natural Sciences
Religious or Ethical Education
Plastic Arts
Pre-technological Training
Musical Training
Physical Education and Sport

Teachers at EGB level have a middle-grade university qualification. They receive their three-year training at University Training Schools for EGB Teachers, during which time they study core subjects of a pedagogical nature, and one special subject in the fields of pre-school teaching, therapeutical pedagogy, the humanities or science (these last in order to teach subjects at the second stage).

Numbers and results

The number of *pupils* at EGB level in the academic year 1982-83 was 5 633 518, which represents 100 per cent of the population between the ages of 6 and 14. Of these, 63.3 per cent attended state schools and the rest, private schools. The number of EGB *schools* is 19 623, of which 14 514 are state schools, and the rest are private. From this one can deduce that private schools are on the average larger than state schools.

From 1970 onwards a policy of "concentration of pupils" has been carried out with the object of getting rid of one-teacher schools. This policy, together with school-bussing services, has permitted the elimination of a number of one-teacher schools mainly in rural areas, where children of all ages were taught by one school teacher, and these have been replaced by schools organised into grades. However, about 5 000 one-teacher schools remain, almost all of them state-run.

The number of pupils per class in the EGB schools is, on the average, 31.14. In state schools this figure is slightly lower (29.09) and in private schools it is higher (35.41), which is largely due to the fact that in rural areas, where there are fewer pupils, the only schools are state schools. For this reason, too, the total number of *teachers* (190 926) is unevenly divided between the state sector (65 per cent) and the private sector (35 per cent).

Evaluation of pupil performance is carried out by the teachers on the spot through continuous assessment which is integrated into the educational process itself. Therefore, it must be borne in mind, when school marks are taken as a criterion of *performance*, that the standards of marks in schools are established normatively (that is, the group characteristics of pupils largely determine the scale on which teachers give marks) and that the level expected and the criteria of testing vary from school to school and from teacher to teacher. Bearing this in mind, the figures for success (positive results in all subjects) at the first stage of EGB is around 85 per cent, while in the second stage it is 60 per cent in state schools, and 70.30 per cent in private schools (64.05 per cent altogether).

As for results at the end of EGB, in 1982, 664 557 pupils finished the course, of whom 68 obtained the diploma of *Graduado Escolar* (the rest only obtained the *Certificado de Escolaridad*). In the following year 49 per cent of the pupils who had finished EGB registered for BUP, 38 per cent for vocational education, and 13 per cent dropped out of the education system.

Special education

The name "Special Education" is given to the type of education provided to those children who have physical or psychological disabilities which do not permit them to follow a normal career at school. When the disability is a serious one, these children attend schools which are different from ordinary ones, although the current trend is towards as much integration as possible, and as time goes by there are in ordinary EGB schools more and more special classrooms and teachers who are specialists in therapeutical teaching. Distributed over specific Special Education Schools, and special classrooms in ordinary schools, there are 98 014 pupils, and approximately half of these are in special schools, and half in ordinary ones. Overall, participation by the private sector in this type of education is very small (8 per cent), although in its Special Education Schools it caters for a majority, 70 per cent.

Almost 70 per cent of the total numbers registered as handicapped consist of children with psychic disorders, while the remaining 30 per cent have different types of physical disabilities. Of these, pupils with hearing handicaps make up 10 per cent; those who suffer from motor deficiencies account for something under 7 per cent, and the blind and those with impaired vision account for some 2 per cent. These children are taught by teachers most of whom are specialising in therapeutical pedagogy and assisted by multi-professional back-up teams consisting of doctors, social workers, psychologists, physiotherapists, and others.

The struggle for human rights has brought about the birth, basically from outside the educational institutions, of a philosophy which tends towards the de-institutionalisation of Special Education, and which demands the total reform of schools, so that disabled children may be incorporated into them. To this end, the Social Integration of the Handicapped Act of 1982 was passed, with the object of effectively incorporating handicapped pupils into the normal school environment. This process of integration has begun, but is taking place very gradually, as it requires a series of measures to be taken vis-à-vis the reform of normal schools: reinforcing their technical resources, introducing specialised teaching staff and inter-disciplinary equipment, modernising the training of the teachers and so on.

Post-compulsory secondary education *(Enseñanzas Medias)*

Training of an academic nature; BUP and COU

The "Unified Polyvalent Bachillerato" (BUP) dates from 1970, although it was in fact implemented for the first time in 1975-76. The General Education Act ascribes a double objective to the *Bachillerato*: to prepare pupils for eventual access to higher studies or to Vocational Education 2 and to give them the necessary training so that they can pass directly on to working life. Thus, there is an express need for it to avoid the excessively theoretical and academic attitude which used to dominate this level of education, and to offer the pupil some variety of practical and professional experience.

The qualification of *Bachillerato* is obtained after passing all the subjects in the three years that make up BUP, there being no final examination. It qualifies the pupil to proceed to university studies (after the University Orientation Course) or to pass on to Vocational Education 2 or (in theory) to do certain types of middle-grade jobs which only require this qualification. In actual fact, however, BUP is simply regarded as a "bridge" to university. Almost all pupils who obtain the *Bachillerato* go to university studies, or at least try to do so, that is, they sit the selective examinations.

The *University Orientation Course* (COU) is an intermediary course between secondary education and higher studies, access to which is gained through the *Bachillerato* or the second level of Vocational Education.

Academic organisation of BUP and COU: curriculum and teachers

The General Education Act of 1970 established, in BUP, a division into core subjects, to be studied by all pupils, optional subjects, with a choice of several, and technical-vocational

THE CURRICULUM OF 1st AND 2nd YEARS OF BUP

Subjects	Hours per week	
	1st year	2nd year
Spanish, Language and Literature*	5	5
Foreign Language**	5	4
Latin	–	4
History	4	–
Geography	–	3
Mathematics	5	4
Natural Sciences	5	–
Physics and Chemistry	–	5
Drawing	3	–
Music and Artistic Activities	2	–
Technical-Professional Studies and Activities	–	2
Religious or Ethical Training	2	2
Physical Education	2	2
Total	33	31

* Since 1978 the study of the vernacular language of those Autonomous Regions with their own language has been incorporated.
** As foreign languages the following can be studied: English, French, German, Italian and Portuguese. (These are in order of frequency of study, there being a great difference between the first two and the rest). The school decides which languages are studied. Some schools offer a choice between two or more languages.

studies, from which the pupil chooses one course. However, the optional subjects are limited to the 3rd year, and grouped into two blocks, in such a way that individual choice is in fact considerably restricted, and the technical studies have been reduced to a very narrow field (Drawing or Domestic Science) studied for two hours a week during the 2nd and 3rd years of the course. Thus the "polyvalence" of the BUP exists in little more than name, and in practice it is just the academic branch of secondary education.

THE CURRICULUM OF THE 3rd YEAR OF BUP

Subjects			Hours per week
Common		Foreign Languages	3
		Geography and History**	5
		Philosophy**	4
		Technical-Professional Activities and Training	2
		Religious or Ethical Education	2
		Physical Education	2
Optional*	Option A	Spanish, Language and Literature	4
		Latin	4
		Greek	4
		Mathematics	4
	Option B	Spanish, Language and Literature	4
		Natural Sciences	4
		Physics and Chemistry	4
		Mathematics	4
Total			30

* Pupils have to choose three subjects from one of the groups A or B. Those choosing Option B do not normally opt for Spanish, and those taking up Option A and including Mathematics are quite rare, too. Thus in practice the two Options correspond to Arts and Sciences.

** In 1979 the curriculum began to include studies known as 'Knowledge of the Constitutional Ordinances', under the authority of the departments of Philosophy and Geography and History.

The University Orientation Course, as befits a course of an intermediary nature, is both the responsibility of the university, which has to devise its programmes and supervise it, and of the *Bachillerato* schools and centres, which have the responsibility of actually giving the course. However, in practice the university takes little part in the programming and orientation and only makes its presence felt in the tests for access to university which the student has to pass at the end of the course. Thus, the idea of individual guidance and of a controlled transition from secondary to higher studies has become completely misrepresented, and nowadays, COU, in general, is in effect just one more year of *Bachillerato*, except that it prepares specifically for the selective tests. In other words, its curriculum is very similar to that of the 3rd year of BUP.

Bachillerato teachers must have a high-grade university degree, normally in the discipline which they teach, although very often they may teach related subjects (for example, a mathematics teacher may teach physics or a philosophy teacher languages) and very occasionally subjects which have nothing to do with their speciality. The education which these

CURRICULUM OF THE UNIVERSITY ORIENTATION COURSE

Subjects				Hours per week
Common		Foreign Language		3
		Philosophy		4
		Spanish Language Seminar		3
Optional	Option A	*a)*	Compulsory Subjects	
			Literature	4
			History of the Modern World	4
		b)	Optional Subjects	
			Latin	4
			Greek	4
			History of Art	4
			Mathematics	4
	Option B	*a)*	Compulsory Subjects	
			Mathematics	4
			Physics	4
		b)	Optional Subjects	
			Chemistry	4
			Biology	4
			Geology	4
			Technical Drawing	4
Total				26

teachers receive at university is of an academic nature, and their actual training as teachers is minimal (acquired through courses at Institutes of Educational Sciences, which are not compulsory for *Bachillerato* teachers) or totally non-existent.

Numbers and results

The number of BUP and COU *pupils* during the academic year 1982-83 was 1 117 600. Two-thirds of these studied at state schools or institutions, and the remaining third in private ones. The number of COU students was 384 018, of whom 71 per cent studied at state establishments (for many private schools do not offer COU).

The average percentage of children between 14 and 16 who study BUP is 37.5 per cent. The figure for 17-year-olds studying COU is somewhat lower (33.8 per cent).

In terms of actual *schools*, the situation is the reverse of that in EGB; the percentage of state schools is lower (45 per cent), even though they actually admit a greater number of pupils. This means that the capacity of the state schools is in general greater than that of the private schools. The total number of schools is 2 495.

The total number of *teachers* in BUP and COU is 45 648, of whom 65 per cent work in state and the rest in private education. The pupil/teacher ratio is 17.2 in the public sector, and 16.5 in the private sector. But these figures could lead to misinterpretation, because, in the *Bachillerato*, there is a greater degree of specialisation by subject, so that the situation is not similar to EGB where the pupil/teacher ratio is normally the same as the number of pupils per class. In fact, here there is a great deal of disparity between the two ratios, since the average number of pupils in a group is 35.6 in the state schools and 35 in the private schools.

As far as *performance* is concerned, the most general evaluation of the efficiency of the system can be obtained by comparing the number of pupils who start BUP with the number of those who finish. In 1982, the number of pupils finishing BUP was exactly half of those who had started three years previously. Of the other 50 per cent, half again had abandoned their studies altogether, and the other half was taking one additional year, or even more, to finish them.

Vocational education *(Formación Profesional, FP)*

Vocational Education was defined by the General Education Act of 1970 as a combination of studies having as its objective the preparation of young people for working life, and was subdivided into three levels:

Level 1: a two-year course leading up to the *Técnico Auxiliar* diploma.

Level 2: a two- or three-year course for pupils who have completed BUP or Level 1. Completion of the course confers the diploma of *Técnico Especialista*.

Level 3: intended to be at the top level of vocational training, this level has not been created.

Organisation of vocational education: curricula and teachers

The curriculum of Level 1 is made up of three areas of knowledge: core subjects, applied sciences and technical and practical studies, these last diversified into different professional branches, of which there are 21. The intention is to provide general training for the pupil as well as specific training for one profession.

CURRICULUM OF LEVEL 1

Areas	Subjects	Hours per week	
		1st year	2nd year
Comon Subjects	Spanish	2	2
	Modern Languages	1	2
	Social Studies [1]	2	3
	Religious or Ethical Studies	2	1
	Physical Education/Sport	1	1
Applied Sciences	Mathematics	2*	2 or 3
	Physics and Chemistry	2**	2 or 3
	Natural Sciences	1**	1 or 2
Technical/ Practical Studies	Technical Drawing and Communications Techniques	3	2 or 3
	Technology	3	3
	Practical	9	9
	Total	28	30

* Common.
** Separate.
1. After 1979, Knowledge of Constitutional Statutes was included in this subject.

Level *2 is organised on the lines of the Bachillerato* and offers the opportunity to acquire specific vocational skills. Within Level 2 there are two separate curricular options, general studies (two years), and specialised training (three), with different programmes. The first of these attracts 5 per cent of the students, and the second, the remaining 95 per cent, which indicates a strong vocational tendency.

The curriculum of the Level 2 general studies programme bears a certain resemblance to that of Level 1 and is also divided into three areas. The specialised training scheme varies according to the branch in question.

Vocational Education *teachers* who teach theoretical subjects have the same university qualifications as those who prepare for the *Bachillerato*, while those who teach practical subjects hold only a Level 2 diploma in the appropriate subject.

Numbers and results

In the academic year 1982-83, 650 929 *pupils* were registered, 65 per cent of whom were in Level 1. The current proportion of the 14-19 year-old age group following this type of course is 17 per cent.

As far as vocational *schools* and institutions are concerned, of the 2 366 in existence, only 42.3 per cent are state-run, although almost 60 per cent of the total number of pupils attend them. There are 42 174 vocational education teachers, which gives a pupil/teacher ratio of 15/1.

Performance at Level 1 is quite low. In 1982, 42.3 per cent of pupils who had started the course two years earlier, finished it. So, there is a high level of dropping out and repeating. In Level 2 the success rate is considerably higher, 68.2 per cent of the pupils finishing their studies within the required time.

University education

Contrary to its provisions for the other educational levels, the General Education Act of 1970 did not prescribe any great reform of university education, either in terms of methodology or of programmes. The only noteworthy innovations were the endowment of university status upon certain types of professional study which did not enjoy it previously (training of primary school teachers and middle-grade technical degrees) and the structuring of university education into three cycles conferring three different types of degree: *diplomado, licenciado* and *doctor*).

There are two types of study within university education:

- One-cycle courses, provided by the *Escuelas Universitarias*, University Schools, which last for three years, with some exceptions, and which lead to the degrees of *Diplomado, Arquitecto Técnico* or *Ingeniero Técnico*.
- Three-cycle courses which are offered in Faculties or Higher Technical Schools. The first cycle is devoted to the study of the basic disciplines and lasts for three years. The second two-year cycle is one of specialisation. The third cycle involves further specialisation and prepares for research and teaching.

Access to the second cycle is open to students who have completed the first cycle and to those who have the degree of *Diplomado* from a University School or the *Arquitectos Técnicos* or *Ingenieros Técnicos*. Anyone successfully completing the second cycle obtains the degree of *Licenciado, Ingeniero* or *Arquitecto*, which qualifies for professional practice and for access to the third cycle. Successful completion of this, and the writing of a thesis which is approved, earns the title of *Doctor*.

The first-cycle studies provided by the Faculties and Higher Technical Schools (ETS) can also be followed in the University Colleges, under the supervision and the regulations of the university to which they belong.

Would-be university students have to fulfil certain academic requirements, and to pass certain tests, according to the nature of the studies previously undertaken and the type of university institution in which they wish to study. As a general rule, all candidates must have successfully completed their secondary education, except for those who are over 25 years of age and who wish to make use of the provision made available to them by law, and have passed a selection test. This gives them the right to register at the university, although they will not necessarily be able to do so in the course of their choice, as this will depend on the capacity of the institution in question and on the academic qualifications of the student.

Enrolment figures

University expansion has been common to a greater or lesser degree to all western nations, and in Spain, in the last ten years, university matriculation has doubled. Correspondingly, therefore, the number of students in higher education per 10 000 inhabitants has grown from the 97.8 at which it stood at the time when the General Education Act was passed in 1970, to 173.4 in the academic year 1980-81.

One primary consideration concerning enrolment figures in higher education is that the students are not evenly distributed, and this is equally valid for all three of the main kinds of study available – Faculties, Higher Technical Schools and University Schools – as well as for state and private provision (the latter only accounts for 3 per cent), and for geographical areas and for the various subjects studied. The tendency for certain universities, as for example those of Madrid or Barcelona, and for certain courses, to account for a high percentage of applications is the reason why one cannot speak of mass enrolments across the board. The problem is largely brought about by the unequal distribution of students among the universities.

A majority of two-thirds register with the faculties, a total of 598 589 students altogether. Registration in the Higher Technical Schools shows a clear downward trend in relative terms: in 1980-81 it was 7.1 per cent; the actual number of their enrolments has not dropped significantly, but the new influx of students has tended to go to the Faculties or the University Schools. With the exception of Architecture, the Higher Technical Schools have not suffered the negative effect of high student enrolments. Finally, the University Schools admit 30 per cent of the students.

The Faculties which have undergone the greatest increases in matriculation have been Economics, Philosophy and Letters (Arts), Medicine, Pharmacy and Law; moreover, matriculation in Biology, probably because it serves as an escape route for those who fail to get into Medicine (for which there is "numerus clausus") in the first instance was, in 1980, five times greater than it had been in 1970-71.

The growth in the number of university students over the last decade is due to various factors: the increase in the number of pupils completing secondary education, and eligible for admission; reclassification of certain types of study which were not previously considered as university studies; the increase in the number of young women applying for admission. In 1980-81, 44 per cent of university students were women, the majority of whom tended to apply for the Faculties or the University Schools; only 9.32 per cent of students registering in the Higher Technical schools were women. However, typically masculine degree courses such as Law or Medicine are now attracting more women.

Naturally, the number of university teachers has also increased during this period; in 1980 there were 40 321. However, one of the biggest obstacles to carrying out any kind of rational planning of university education has been, until now, the existence of a multitude of different types of status, whether in terms of category – professors, lecturers, assistant-lecturers or junior lecturers; or tenure – permanent, interim or contractual; or commitment – part-time, half-time or full-time.

University autonomy and the University Reform Act (LRU)

The principle of university autonomy is enshrined in the Constitution, which aimed at revising the traditional, centralised, administrative and legal régime of the university. However, the need for university reform does not stem merely from constitutional development. It also stems from the deep-seated nature of the complaints with which the institutions are afflicted and from a political determination to face up to them. It is also true to say that every process of renewal in Spanish society and of democratisation of its political life has of necessity raised the question of modernising the universities.

The biggest problems facing the universities today are the following:

– In terms of their functions – the predominance of specialisation and the decline of formative and cultural objectives.
– The mushrooming of the university population over a very short time which has led to:
  • problems in terms of the numbers and quality of teachers
  • problems relating to facilities and adequate equipment
  • problems of teaching methods
  • lack of a coherent educational policy
  • lack of planning, at least in the medium term
  • high drop-out and failure rates.

In order to solve all these problems while observing the principle of university autonomy, the University Reform Act (LRU) was passed in 1983. The Act established a framework for the future organisation and structure of higher education, granting each university responsibility for deciding what model of higher education to offer, so that each one can integrate its own special characteristics in drawing up regulations and fulfilling, observing and implementing the provisions of the Act.

4. EDUCATIONAL POLICY: FUTURE PROSPECTS

Although in describing the education system we have already referred to some of the deficiencies of the system, and to the projects for reform which are being developed, it seems a good idea to end this summary with as systematic as possible an account of current educational policy, since it is on the success or failure of this policy that the future of the Spanish education system, like other systems facing up to their own deficiencies and meeting the demands of both the present and future, will finally depend.

The education policy, the general outlines of which we shall examine in this section, is, of course, that of the present government. Even when the comparative newness of this policy has been stressed, the reader should not forget that the majority of the reforms which are under way are designed to meet needs which are almost universally felt, and to tackle deficiencies about whose causes there is a wide and general consensus. The most important of these reforms are laid down by the Constitution itself, and were in fact begun by earlier governments, as for instance the University Reform Act, the decentralisation of educational administration or free compulsory education.

This section is divided into four major parts. First, the efforts to achieve harmonious collaboration between public and private institutions in order to guarantee the right of all to education is spelt out; the best example of this is the Rights to Education Act, which regulates both the powers of the various public administrations and their relationship with private education. Second, programmes to correct inequality of opportunity. Third, reforms designed to improve the quality of education. Fourth, university reform.

The Rights to Education Act and the legal framework of non-university education

The Rights to Education Act, passed by Parliament in 1983, has yet to come into force, pending the outcome of certain appeals against it which are at present before the Constitutional Tribunal. The controversy surrounding this Act stems from the fact that it affects both state and private education and attempts to abolish the traditional split in the education system by setting up an integrated network of state and other schools under the co-ordination of public authorities.

The primary objective of the Act may be considered to be the integration of all teaching establishments into a combined, completely coherent and organised network, which will ensure that the right of everyone to education is respected, as laid down in the Constitution. With this integrated network it should be possible, in the first instance, to trace a kind of *carte scolaire* (school map), which will permit rational planning of resources, standardization of working conditions in all schools maintained with public money and deal with such matters as participation, recruitment of teachers and provision of free education.

The second objective is to harmonize the diverse aspects of freedom of education. Of these, the main ones are to establish and run schools, teachers' freedom in the classroom, the freedom of pupils to learn, and the freedom of parents to choose a school for their children.

A third aim of the Act is the participation of parents in the internal life of the school as well as that of teachers and pupils, so that parents' rights do not stop at the school gate, and so that closer links may be established between education as given in the school and in the family. The proprietors of private schools think that participation is going too far when it is extended to the School Board (a body consisting of the headteacher, teachers, parents and pupils over 12) which can select the headteacher and control the selection of teachers.

The participation of all interested parties in the general planning of education (Article 27.5 of the Constitution) is regulated under the Rights to Education Act through the State Schooling Board (*Consejo Escolar del Estado*), and other bodies at various levels of government. Although the intention is that all these bodies, from the state level down to the school boards themselves, should limit the role of the public authorities, this Act has been considered "interventionist".

The right of all to education, and the eradication of educational inequality

Social inequality in Spain has two serious aspects: inequality of condition, and inequality of opportunity. The influence of social origins on the lives of individuals in Spain has, throughout this century, been twice that in England and three times greater than in the United States. Education has, everywhere, an ambivalent tendency, either that of passing on social inequality, or that of levelling it out. In Spain it has been mostly the former. Educational inequality is a direct and immediate reflection, without any academic validity or justification, of economic and social inequality.

It follows that what is understood by equality of opportunity is simply an aspect of the right of all to education, and this has important implications for policies at different levels of education. In the words of the Minister of Education himself:

The search for equality does not consist in giving the same things to those who feel they are unequal. Real equality of opportunity does not require a free and undifferentiated offer of education at all levels, the costs to be borne by the public purse. To put it another way, the search for equity through equality of educational opportunity takes a different form at the levels which the laws define as mandatory than it does at the post-compulsory stage.

When education is compulsory, it should aspire to an equality of outcomes... the principle of equality demands that no one be discriminated against or hindered in his educatonal advancement through lack of economic means. The aim at these post-compulsory levels, whether they provide secondary or university education, is not equality of outcomes but equality of opportunity.

At the compulsory level, each little boy or girl, wherever he or she lives, whatever the social condition of their family, should have a right to a basic education through a free and worthwhile place in school. At the post-compulsory level, the right to education means being able to take full advantage of the education system and its facilities, according to personal capacity and intellectual effort. At these levels, equality of opportunity does not consist in a generalised offer of free places, but in individualised support through a grants system.

• In the programme of the present government, pride of place is given to the generalisation of schooling from the age of 4 to the age of 16. To achieve this it is necessary to increase the supply of school places.

Schooling for the entire age group having been attained in Basic General Education, investment at that level will be restricted to replacing schools in a poor condition; this should make it possible to devote resources to the other levels. Up to and including 1986 the buildings and facilities required for more than 250 000 school places will be provided and these should be enough to cover the needs of children between 4 and 5 years old. The creation of between 200 000 and 300 000 school places at secondary school level is also foreseen, depending on the progress of the reforms being carried out and on the availability of budgetary resources. This rate of construction and equipping of school facilities, with the accompanying increase in teacher numbers, will make it possible to fulfil the aim of the generalisation of schooling to all children between 4 and 16 years old. However, there will still be some holes and gaps to fill and some *ad hoc* programmes will be necessary.

• The present government has set in motion a Compensatory Education Programme, which is closer to the ZEP (Educational Priority Zones) in France than to programmes with a similar name in other countries. This programme has been conceived as an emergency measure to remedy the educational situation in the more forgotten areas or among depressed social groups, with special attention being paid to outlying or rural districts and to young people of 14 or 15 who do not attend school.

• At the post-compulsory level, a grants policy is the main instrument the public authorities can apply to bring about equality of opportunity. The support system has been adjusted in several ways: first, grants are being concentrated at post-compulsory levels (secondary and university); secondly, priority is being given to families on low incomes; thirdly, controls are being introduced to prevent fraudulent declarations of income; fourthly, a relationship between the amount of grant and the minimum legal wage is being established to ensure that the grant maintains its purchasing power; fifthly, resources being channelled into grants will be increased to 76 per cent.

At university level, the present government is implementing a joint policy of grants and fees. Academic fees cover 20 per cent of the cost of studies. Given the class-ridden nature of the university, and the uncertain progress of the Spanish fiscal system, the rest is being paid mainly by those who do not go to university. This situation is without doubt unequal and contrary to the principle of transfers; it can be remedied by raising fees and, at the same time, grants for students from low income families.

• Another programme mounted to fight inequality in education is the programme of Adult Education; the needs of lifelong adult education can be estimated as being equivalent to those of formal education. Here, obviously, at the top of the list of potential clients, must be total illiterates, and then semi-literates.

In addition to specific measures connected with the Compensatory Education Programme, mainly undertaken in collaboration with various local authorities and the Autonomous Regions of Andalucia and the Canaries, and with support from the Popular Universities, the present government is radically reshaping adult education, getting rid of its excessively academic slant, and trying to coordinate its activities better.

• Another priority, activity against inequality, whether natural or social, is in the area of Special Education. In this field the intention is to move progressively and carefully along the road towards integration in such a way as to ensure that each case will be catered for appropriately.

The quality of education

After the guarantee for all of the right to education, and removal of educational inequalities, raising the quality of education is the third great aim of current educational policy. The majority of indicators which can be used to measure quality lead us to suppose that quality is low. As far as input is concerned, the unit cost of maintaining a school place is low, and in secondary education the real costs fall far short of the theoretically desirable ones; once the costs of construction and staff are deducted, there is very little left for maintenance and running costs. Furthermore, the teacher/pupil ratio is unusually high. If we accept failure at school as a measure of the quality of output, it is clear that there are too many pupils, at all levels, who fail subjects, have to repeat a year and finally drop out.

Whether these indicators are reliable or not, the truth is that in order to improve the quality of education, one has to increase input and enhance the way in which resources are exploited on the ground by teachers and pupils. A series of reforms and programmes on such lines is being developed at the moment – the focus being on the pupils. In particular, attempts are being made to improve the training of teachers, to improve educational methods, and to strengthen the curriculum by rectifying defects and adapting it to social change.

Action on teachers

As far as both initial and in-service training of teachers are concerned, there are many defects in the present system, and reform is necessary. Whereas projects for the reform of initial training are at present under discussion, and are making slow progress because they overlap with all the university reforms, the reform of in-service training is making smoother progress; in fact, a decree was signed in November 1984, setting up Teacher Training Centres, the first of which was to come into operation before the start of the following academic year. At the moment the situation lies somewhere between the old *Institutos de las*

Ciencias de Educación, which will continue to function within the universities, and the new Training Centres.

Policy on staff is tending, first, to subordinate the special mobility of state teachers to the needs of the schools and towards the constitution of stable pedagogical groups; second, to increase motivation and performance of teachers through the structuring of an education degree programme. On the one hand, the recasting into two categories (*Maestros* and Secondary Teachers) out of the 26 classes and levels of teachers existing at the moment will facilitate horizontal movement; on the other hand, vertical channels are being opened up, not only in the varying scales and intervals between the two new categories, but also between the different levels of teaching.

Action on methods and technology

Programmes of considerable scope have been set up by some Autonomous Regions for the introduction of new technology into education; at the same time, the Ministry of Education itself is promoting this nationwide.

The Atenea Project, for the introduction of microcomputers into education, was to be carried through late in 1985, and it is expected that it will last for five years. In its current version, the equipping of 1 800 schools with more than 9 000 machines is envisaged, as well as the training of 5 500 teachers, and the subsequent specialisation of nearly 1 300 of them; in addition there are translation and production of software schemes under way in collaboration with other European and South American countries. There is also a more modest project, co-ordinated by a Ministerial Commission on Audo-Visual Materials, to promote the use of audio-visual material, and especially video, in education. Lastly, both the programmes of teacher training and the reforms in the curricula at various levels of education emphasize the enormous importance of methodology in teaching.

Curriculum reform

The modernisation and adaptation of curricula and syllabuses is, as with methodology, one of the basic objectives of the reforms undertaken at the various levels of education outside university.

• Preliminary work on a Bill for infant schools is being carried out, which will deal, in a single piece of legislation, with the educational, social and health needs of the smallest children. The model for infant schools is oriented towards the active development of the child's possibilities in such a way that, from the very outset of the educational cycle, the causes which lead to social and cultural inequality are tackled.

• The reform of EGB requires, in the opinion of the present government, a re-orientation of the changes which were gradually introduced after 1981. The entry into force of the programmes for the upper cycle of EGB having been suspended, a systematic evaluation was made of the results achieved by the first set of pupils completing the initial cycle of EGB, and the opinions of teachers on the new system were canvassed.

As a result of this, the Ministry is readjusting once more the minumum levels in the programmes of the initial and middle cycles, and carefully and progressively designing a new curriculum for the upper cycle. A first phase of experimentation, during the academic year 1984-85, is designed to evaluate the degree of mastery of the proposed terminal objectives, to promote a new, active methodology for the teachers, and to identify needs in relation to pedagogical resources and teacher training. The experiment as such will actually begin in the academic year 1985-86, and it is envisaged that it will be generalised at the same time as the reform of secondary education.

- As far as the reform of secondary education is concerned, the diagnosis is clear. BUP was conceived in the General Education Act as a cycle of education with little purpose other than that of giving access to university. Since 1970 it has become a very traditional cycle, with curricula and methodology which are not particularly up-to-date. The teacher/pupil ratio is very high in some schools, while technical education has not been sufficiently developed, and, in general, the academic nature of education is very highly emphasized. On the other hand, the conversion of the University Orientation Course into a mere prolongation of BUP, designed to prepare students for university entrance, has accentuated the non-functional nature of a cycle which does not prepare people for employment, and the main objective of which is to be a one-way path to higher studies. The binary structure which has developed is not only unfair but does not work too well: it is in vocational education that there is the highest number of drop-outs and scholastic failure.

Attempts are being made to raise the school-leaving age to 16, though the authorities are fully aware that the ills of the education system are not going to be remedied with more of the same. In order that schooling be worthy of the name, it is necessary to find a solution which can overcome the deficiencies of Basic General Education and of the first two years of secondary education in their present form; it will also be necessary to make up the lack of school places, and to stimulate demand for education since, at the present time, more that 200 000 young people of 14 and 15 are not attending any kind of school; these problems will shortly be dealt with by the Compensatory Education Programme. The aim in the medium term, over the next 6 to 8 years, is to establish an initial cycle of secondary education from 12 to 16 years of age, similar to that obtaining in other European countries. Then, for some pupils, there would be a *Bachillerato* course which would lead to university or qualify for vocational training, the redesign of which has hardly begun.

During the academic year 1983-84, experiments have begun with secondary education in the area of what would be the upper cycle, that is, for the time being, the two years immediately following Basic General Education (14 to 15).

The main characteristics of the new curricular outline are:

- Integral and "polyvalent" training (unifying academic and technical education in one free, compulsory cycle).
- A terminal nature (preparation of the young person for everyday life given that it does not lead on to higher studies).
- The linking of studies to the pupils' environment by means of decentralisation and giving greater flexibility to the content.
- Active methodology, with the implied changes in the teacher-pupil relationship.

The experimental plan for reform has been conceived as a gradual process. The upper cycle reform has been initiated in a small number of schools; certain modifications have been introduced into their programmes and other curricular activities. Later on, the number of schools involved in the experiment will be increased until the reform is generalised, by 1988-89. Naturally, this would incorporate such modifications as continuous assessment may make necessary. Experimentation with the second cycle will begin in 1985-86, and the outcome will be a *Bachillerato* course with three options (academic, artistic and technical) while the University Orientation Course will be dropped.

University reform

As has already been stated, university reform has begun with the University Reform Act of August 1983. The most noteworthy innovations as a result of the Act are:

a) The right of each university to define, independently, its own regulations.
b) Institutional autonomy in financing and management.
c) The institutionalisation of a Social Council which will enable the participation of the community in the governance of each university.
d) Departmental structure: the department becomes the focus of the thrust of university reform.
e) Autonomy and greater flexibility of curricula.
f) Simplification of teaching categories and stability of the teaching staff.

Since the Act was passed, the universities have formed new governing councils and senates, some of which are already making their own regulations. An Act has been passed mandating a "Social Council" for each university and the national Universities Council as a co-ordinating body for them all. Prior to the summer of 1984 "suitability tests" were organised, after which contractual teachers were granted tenure, or the opportunity to accept it.

Through successive decrees, agreements between university departments with companies, definition of areas of knowledge or disciplines, the setting-up of departments, studies in the third cycle and other aspects of higher education requiring legislation have been endowed with a legal basis. At present the rules governing access to university are being studied, as well as a curricular framework. Initial steps are also being taken to transfer responsibility for the universities to the Autonomous Regions in which each is situated. In short, relatively unhindered progress is being made along the road to autonomy, the modernisation of academic structures and a functional connection between the universities and their social environment.

OECD SALES AGENTS
DÉPOSITAIRES DES PUBLICATIONS DE L'OCDE

ARGENTINA - ARGENTINE
Carlos Hirsch S.R.L.,
Florida 165, 4º Piso,
(Galeria Guemes) 1333 Buenos Aires
Tel. 33.1787.2391 y 30.7122

AUSTRALIA-AUSTRALIE
D.A. Book (Aust.) Pty. Ltd.
11-13 Station Street (P.O. Box 163)
Mitcham, Vic. 3132   Tel. (03) 873 4411

AUSTRIA - AUTRICHE
OECD Publications and Information Centre,
4 Simrockstrasse,
5300 Bonn (Germany)   Tel. (0228) 21.60.45
Local Agent:
Gerold & Co., Graben 31, Wien 1 Tel. 52.22.35

BELGIUM - BELGIQUE
Jean de Lannoy, Service Publications OCDE,
avenue du Roi 202
B-1060 Bruxelles   Tel. 02/538.51.69

CANADA
Renouf Publishing Company Limited/
Éditions Renouf Limitée Head Office/
Siège social – Store/Magasin :
61, rue Sparks Street,
Ottawa, Ontario K1P 5A6
        Tel. (613)238-8985. 1-800-267-4164
Store/Magasin : 211, rue Yonge Street,
Toronto, Ontario M5B 1M4.
        Tel. (416)363-3171
Regional Sales Office/
Bureau des Ventes régional :
7575 Trans-Canada Hwy., Suite 305,
Saint-Laurent, Quebec H4T 1V6
        Tel. (514)335-9274

DENMARK - DANEMARK
Munksgaard Export and Subscription Service
35, Nørre Søgade, DK-1370 København K
        Tel. +45.1.12.85.70

FINLAND - FINLANDE
Akateeminen Kirjakauppa,
Keskuskatu 1, 00100 Helsinki 10 Tel. 0.12141

FRANCE
OCDE/OECD
Mail Orders/Commandes par correspondance :
2, rue André-Pascal,
75775 Paris Cedex 16
        Tel. (1) 45.24.82.00
Bookshop/Librairie : 33, rue Octave-Feuillet
75016 Paris
        Tel. (1) 45.24.81.67 ou/ou (1) 45.24.81.81
Principal correspondant :
Librairie de l'Université,
12a, rue Nazareth,
13602 Aix-en-Provence   Tel. 42.26.18.08

GERMANY - ALLEMAGNE
OECD Publications and Information Centre,
4 Simrockstrasse,
5300 Bonn   Tel. (0228) 21.60.45

GREECE - GRÈCE
Librairie Kauffmann,
28, rue du Stade, 105 64 Athens Tel. 322.21.60

HONG KONG
Government Information Services,
Publications (Sales) Office,
Beaconsfield House, 4/F.,
Queen's Road Central

ICELAND - ISLANDE
Snæbjörn Jónsson & Co., h.f.,
Hafnarstræti 4 & 9,
P.O.B. 1131 – Reykjavik
        Tel. 13133/14281/11936

INDIA - INDE
Oxford Book and Stationery Co.,
Scindia House, New Delhi 1   Tel. 45896
17 Park St., Calcutta 700016   Tel. 240832

INDONESIA - INDONESIE
Pdii-Lipi, P.O. Box 3065/JKT.Jakarta
        Tel. 583467

ITALY - ITALIE
Libreria Commissionaria Sansoni,
Via Lamarmora 45, 50121 Firenze
        Tel. 579751/584468
Via Bartolini 29, 20155 Milano Tel. 365083
Sub-depositari :
Ugo Tassi, Via A. Farnese 28,
00192 Roma   Tel. 310590
Editrice e Libreria Herder,
Piazza Montecitorio 120, 00186 Roma
        Tel. 6794628
Agenzia Libraria Pegaso,
Via de Romita 5, 70121 Bari
        Tel. 540.105/540.195
Agenzia Libraria Pegaso, Via S.Anna dei
Lombardi 16, 80134 Napoli. Tel. 314180
Libreria Hœpli,
Via Hœpli 5, 20121 Milano Tel. 865446
Libreria Scientifica
Dott. Lucio de Biasio "Aeiou"
Via Meravigli 16, 20123 Milano Tel. 807679
Libreria Zanichelli, Piazza Galvani 1/A,
40124 Bologna   Tel. 237389
Libreria Lattes,
Via Garibaldi 3, 10122 Torino Tel. 519274
La diffusione delle edizioni OCSE è inoltre
assicurata dalle migliori librerie nelle città più
importanti.

JAPAN - JAPON
OECD Publications and Information Centre,
Landic Akasaka Bldg., 2-3-4 Akasaka,
Minato-ku, Tokyo 107   Tel. 586.2016

KOREA - CORÉE
Pan Korea Book Corporation
P.O.Box No. 101 Kwangwhamun, Seoul
        Tel. 72.7369

LEBANON - LIBAN
Documenta Scientifica/Redico,
Edison Building, Bliss St.,
P.O.B. 5641, Beirut   Tel. 354429-344425

MALAYSIA - MALAISIE
University of Malaya Co-operative Bookshop
Ltd.,
P.O.Box 1127, Jalan Pantai Baru,
Kuala Lumpur   Tel. 577701/577072

NETHERLANDS - PAYS-BAS
Staatsuitgeverij
Chr. Plantijnstraat, 2 Postbus 20014
2500 EA S-Gravenhage   Tel. 070-789911
Voor bestellingen: Tel. 070-789880

NEW ZEALAND - NOUVELLE-ZÉLANDE
Government Printing Office Bookshops:
Auckland: Retail Bookshop, 25 Rutland Street,
Mail Orders, 85 Beach Road
Private Bag C.P.O.
Hamilton: Retail: Ward Street,
Mail Orders, P.O. Box 857
Wellington: Retail, Mulgrave Street, (Head
Office)
Cubacade World Trade Centre,
Mail Orders, Private Bag
Christchurch: Retail, 159 Hereford Street,
Mail Orders, Private Bag
Dunedin: Retail, Princes Street,
Mail Orders, P.O. Box 1104

NORWAY - NORVÈGE
Tanum-Karl Johan
Karl Johans gate 43, Oslo 1
PB 1177 Sentrum, 0107 Oslo 1Tel. (02) 42.93.10

PAKISTAN
Mirza Book Agency
65 Shahrah Quaid-E-Azam, Lahore 3 Tel. 66839

PORTUGAL
Livraria Portugal,
Rua do Carmo 70-74, 1117 Lisboa Codex.
        Tel. 360582/3

SINGAPORE - SINGAPOUR
Information Publications Pte Ltd
Pei-Fu Industrial Building,
24 New Industrial Road No. 02-06
Singapore 1953   Tel. 2831786, 2831798

SPAIN - ESPAGNE
Mundi-Prensa Libros, S.A.,
Castelló 37, Apartado 1223, Madrid-28001
        Tel. 431.33.99
Libreria Bosch, Ronda Universidad 11,
Barcelona 7   Tel. 317.53.08/317.53.58

SWEDEN - SUÈDE
AB CE Fritzes Kungl. Hovbokhandel,
Box 16356, S 103 27 STH,
Regeringsgatan 12,
DS Stockholm   Tel. (08) 23.89.00
Subscription Agency/Abonnements:
Wennergren-Williams AB,
Box 30004, S104 25 Stockholm. Tel. 08/54.12.00

SWITZERLAND - SUISSE
OECD Publications and Information Centre,
4 Simrockstrasse,
5300 Bonn (Germany)   Tel. (0228) 21.60.45
Local Agent:
Librairie Payot,
6 rue Grenus, 1211 Genève 11
        Tel. (022) 31.89.50

TAIWAN - FORMOSE
Good Faith Worldwide Int'l Co., Ltd.
9th floor, No. 118, Sec.2
Chung Hsiao E. Road
Taipei   Tel. 391.7396/391.7397

THAILAND - THAILANDE
Suksit Siam Co., Ltd.,
1715 Rama IV Rd.,
Samyam Bangkok 5   Tel. 2511630

TURKEY - TURQUIE
Kültur Yayinlari Is-Türk Ltd. Sti.
Atatürk Bulvari No: 191/Kat. 21
Kavaklidere/Ankara   Tel. 25.07.60
Dolmabahce Cad. No: 29
Besiktas/Istanbul   Tel. 160.71.88

UNITED KINGDOM - ROYAUME UNI
H.M. Stationery Office,
Postal orders only:
P.O.B. 276, London SW8 5DT
Telephone orders: (01) 622.3316, or
Personal callers:
49 High Holborn, London WC1V 6HB
Branches at: Belfast, Birmingham,
Bristol, Edinburgh, Manchester

UNITED STATES - ÉTATS-UNIS
OECD Publications and Information Centre,
Suite 1207, 1750 Pennsylvania Ave., N.W.,
Washington, D.C. 20006 - 4582
        Tel. (202) 724.1857

VENEZUELA
Libreria del Este,
Avda F. Miranda 52, Aptdo. 60337,
Edificio Galipan, Caracas 106
        Tel. 32.23.01/33.26.04/31.58.38

YUGOSLAVIA - YOUGOSLAVIE
Jugoslovenska Knjiga, Knez Mihajlova 2,
P.O.B. 36, Beograd   Tel. 621.992

Orders and inquiries from countries where Sales
Agents have not yet been appointed should be sent
to:
OECD, Publications Service, Sales and
Distribution Division, 2, rue André-Pascal, 75775
PARIS CEDEX 16.

Les commandes provenant de pays où l'OCDE n'a
pas encore désigné de dépositaire peuvent être
adressées à :
OCDE, Service des Publications. Division des
Ventes et Distribution. 2, rue André-Pascal. 75775
PARIS CEDEX 16.

70024-10-1986

OECD PUBLICATIONS, 2, rue André-Pascal, 75775 PARIS CEDEX 16 - No. 43789 1986
PRINTED IN FRANCE
(91 87 01 1) ISBN 92-64-12902-2